ON POETRY

ON POETRY:

Jonathan Davidson

smith|doorstop

Published 2018 by
Smith|Doorstop Books
The Poetry Business
Campo House,
54 Campo Lane,
Sheffield S1 2EG
www.poetrybusiness.co.uk

ISBN 978-1-910367-93-3

British Library Cataloguing-in-Publication Data.
A catalogue record for this book is available from the
British Library.

Designed & typeset by Utter
Printed by CPI Books
Author photo: Lee Allen

Smith|Doorstop is a member of Inpress,
www.inpressbooks.co.uk. Distributed by
NBN International, Airport Business Centre,
10 Thornbury Road Plymouth PL 6 7PP.

The Poetry Business receives financial support from
Arts Council England

Contents

For my mum, who gave me poetry.

INTRODUCTION

These essays and pieces of memoir are about my relationship with poetry. I've written about what I heard or read when I was young and some of the poems I've carried with me over the years. My interest in poetry has taken me outside the UK and I'm interested in poetry in translation. I've written about this. I'm interested in what might happen when poetry presents itself to the world – through performance or broadcast – and I've written about this too.

My background – working class and not good at exams – meant that I came to poetry by chance. I was hardly ever forced to read poetry and despite – or because – of this some poems have stayed with me. I've written about how it is to live with certain poems for many years. Poetry is an art-form that carries with it its own means of delivery, its own theatre, concert hall or back room. To speak or even to hear speech in our heads is talent and facility enough to experience poetry. In some pieces I write about this.

I've tried to make up my own mind about what is worth paying attention to and what isn't. Attention is important. There is *some* money in poetry but attention is the currency in which poets are paid. Like any trade it has its coiners and clippers. Reputations are built or launched and stand or fall to earth. I'm interested in what remains when the fuss has died down – the quiet voices. I've written about some of these.

Poetry is simple and complex. It has little *public* worth and gathers very little value in the world. But privately poems take our concentration and consideration and turn this into energy. Poems find themselves in the firmament. They glow when they are of beautiful use, when they are heard and shared, when they are part of the Poetry Commonwealth. And as we've always understood of stars, they are worth gazing at, and sometimes worth following.

– Jonathan Davidson, 2018

CHAPTER 1

The poet Catherine Byron – Ivan V. Lalić in Leicester – Did you know Michael Farley? – A Fawn Overcoat – The Poetry Commonwealth – Changing Trains at Kanfanar – A Russian Poet encourages Glasnost – A non-person from Czechoslovakia opens a door in Scunthorpe – Manon des Sources *begins at the end – Giving a shout – A good man.*

In the mid-1980s the Yugoslavian poet Ivan V. Lalić came to the city of Leicester to give a poetry reading.[1] It was arranged by the poet Catherine Byron and by her then partner, the poet Michael Farley.[2] Ivan V. Lalić died in 1996. I haven't heard of Catherine for a while and I long ago lost contact with Michael.[3] Wherever they are, this little event that they engineered still resonates with me. It was unusual. It was typical. Poets and others gathering in a city in the English Midlands to listen to poetry in its original Serbian and in English translation was unusual. That there were only about a dozen of us there to listen was typical. I was in my early twenties and it was my first experience of poetry in translation and the first time I had met a poet from an *alien* poetic culture. Had I known more about poetry I would have known that there are no alien poetic cultures but my diet had up until then been exclusively the poetry of the English language, and mostly the poetry of English poets. And mostly dead English poets.

Lalić was a poet working beyond the range of my experience. Despite this, I remember watching him take off his belted fawn overcoat at the start of the reading and turning to look at us as if we were already part of his world, as if we were citizens and contributors to a Poetry Commonwealth. And we were. Both.

Lalić was a gentle, quietly spoken man. He was the object of our intense attention but he presented himself modestly, aware that he was a dignified curiosity. If he was concerned about whether his poetry would mean much to us in English translation he didn't let on. Carefully he read the translations and carefully we listened. Each poem was let loose into the room as if at its moment of creation. And for those of us who hardly knew this poet existed, it was as good as hearing the poems at their making. The translations may have been particularly fine, his introduction to each poem may have given us just what we needed, or the background hum of the Leicester inner ring road may have been the perfect incongruous detail. Or perhaps it was that Lalić's poems had something that carried them easily across the disputed kilometres and through the dangerous century. They went from the past into the future. None of us knew then what a broken future it was to be.

I have comes across his poems now and then over the decades that followed, most recently 'The Spaces of Hope' translated from the Serbian by Francis R Jones.[4] This was published in the UK a few years after Lalić's reading in Leicester, but he may have read it in manuscript form. It is a deceptively direct and simple poem. It does not, in translation anyway, rely on poetic sleights of hand or obtuse references – although the details are not entirely universal. It is not a work of imagination so much as a work of reflection. The title, despite being rather abstract, echoes through the poem and gathers meaning. There are some agile phrases. 'A starless night lit only / By a book on the table' is a lovely idea and a lovely image. The poem is a perfect meshing of the facts of the matter with precise analysis of their potential implications.

The Spaces of Hope

by Ivan V. Lalić

I have experienced the spaces of hope,
The spaces of a moderate mercy. Experienced
The places which suddenly set
Into a random form: a lilac garden,
A street in Florence, a morning room,
A sea smeared with silver before the storm,
Or a starless night lit only
By a book on the table. The spaces of hope
Are in time, not linked into
A system of miracles, nor into a unity;
They merely exist. As in Kanfanar,
At the station; wind in a wild vine
A quarter-century ago: one space of hope.
Another, set somewhere in the future,
Is already destroying the void around it,
Unclear but real. Probable.

In the spaces of hope light grows,
Free of charge, and voices are clearer,
Death has a beautiful shadow, the lilac blooms later,
But for that it looks like its first-ever flower.

Lalić was never a familiar name, despite his reading in Leicester, and since his death it is all too easy to assume that his poetry has stopped emitting light. This poem proves this is not the case, it is so powerful still. Sometimes, it is important to read the poems that are furthest from us – in age or geography or cultural background – because what manages to be transmitted across time and space and from language to language, that will be *the poetry*. This is what I want as a reader and listener: from out of the static and white noise, to suddenly receive poetry.

However distant the galaxy – a poem can take hundreds of years for its light to reach us – reach us it may. It demands some work. It can be terribly inconvenient to have to have our satellite dishes constantly turning day and night and to pick out the verse from the interference.

It's an exaggeration to say that as a reader I have preferred to travel on foot and across open country with nothing but the stars for guidance, but I do like to take the back roads. Which is in itself somehow fitting as poetry can be at its most powerful when, having offered us the ambiguity of metaphor and simile, and the formlessness of abstraction, and the beguiling clatter of consonance, and all the many other doors and chambers through which a poem passes, the road rises and the mist suddenly clears and we find ourselves on a hilltop staring at a star we didn't know existed.[5] Re-reading 'The Spaces of Hope' I imagine how Lalić must have set out to discover what this almost gauche abstraction might mean for one who had lived through the Second World War, who had grown up in a country within a country, who knew the bloody uncertainty of history. He might have written a memoir or a history book, but he chose to write poems. And in this instance, he focussed on a street in Florence and the railway station at Kanfanar.[6] And, most tellingly, on little lilac flowers.[7] Things both particular and universal. The poem, created so many years ago, is received. Still. Like light.

Although it was Anvil Press Poetry in the 1980s who were making the work of Lalić available to readers in the UK, it was Bloodaxe Books who did most in my 20s to introduce me to poetry in translation. I was slightly too young to register the impact of the Penguin *Modern Poets in Translation Series* but Bloodaxe continued the work of this series by intercepting and making public the poetry of poets from a politically volatile Eastern Europe. They published, for instance, the Czechoslovakian poet Miroslav Holub and the Romanian poet Marin Sorescu, both of whom wrote from within political systems that seemed to simultaneously celebrate and frustrate poets and poetry. While at Leicester Polytechnic I helped make a performance of the poetry of Russian dissident poet Irina Ratushinskaya, drawn from the collection *No, I'm not afraid*, published by Bloodaxe in 1986. Her story, we reasoned, would be more powerful if her poems were performed. The audience, the performers, the poems and the poet, would all have made a connection. Even if she were imprisoned – as she had been – her poetry could be released. Poetry can make its own moments. It can at least help to change the world.[8]

In the early 1990s I was in the position to invite poets to give readings.[9] The details are hazy, but somehow I arranged for Miroslav Holub to visit the steel making town of Scunthorpe in North Lincolnshire. He read the English translations of his poems and they seemed at the time to be perceptive and wise. Perhaps he wrote with the knowledge that for his work to have an audience beyond that of his small country he would have to be translated, and there is a sense in his best work that nothing has been lost in translation. Here is his poem 'The Door', translated by Ian Milner:[10]

The Door

by Miroslav Holub

Go and open the door.
    Maybe outside there's
    a tree, or a wood,
    a garden,
    or a magic city.

Go and open the door.
    Maybe a dog's rummaging.

Maybe you'll see a face,
or an eye,
or the picture
of a picture.

Go and open the door.
If there's a fog
it will clear.

Go and open the door.
Even if there's only
the darkness ticking,
even if there's only
the hollow wind,
even if
nothing
is there,
go and open the door.

At least
there'll be
a draught.

As with so many poems by Holub, it speaks with a clarity which makes the ambiguity of his intent more powerful. We can assume that for much of his writing life Holub was having to say one thing and mean another.[11] And perhaps his career as a scientist ensured that he wrote with a certain detachment, the better able to present his observations. Certainly this poem is a long way from the personal introspection that marked so much poetry written in the same period in Western Europe. His personality is absent. With good reason. The poet, perhaps, had been asked to step into a side room to have a word with some gentlemen from the Ministry. So we are alone with the poem. Just us and the words. We hear footsteps in the corridor outside and doors opening and closing, but there is just enough time to appreciate the suggestion that the poem offers, that other ways of living are possible and that a country – that individuals – should have the nerve to find out what they might be.

Not long after that reading by Miroslav Holub I went to see the film *Manon des Sources*, screened at the Scunthorpe Film Theatre, then run by my friend Tony Whitehead.[12] This was still the days of films arriving from wherever they had been last shown in a series of shallow tins, each numbered so that the projectionist knew in which order to screen them. Shortly after the opening credits and a bit of Gallic action, we witnessed one of the lead characters, Ugolin, committing suicide by hanging himself from a tree.[13] But that can't be right, we thought, surely that's part of the grim denouement? And then what must have been the next reel was screened and we were somewhere in the middle of the story. We did our best but couldn't make head nor tail of it. Then the screen went dark. Tony came on the address system to say that the reels had been mixed up by the clots at the Grimsby Film Theatre so he was just going to have to screen them one by one and could we give him a shout when it all made sense. It took four hours but it was an oddly profound experience. Which is what writing poetry may be about, just giving a shout if we think, even momentarily, that it all makes sense. Which was what Ivan V. Lalić was doing, that evening in Leicester. And what I still listen out for.

1 This was before the Yugoslavian wars of succession in the 1990s.

2 Catherine Byron was the first published poet I met, at the age of 21. She was also the first person to refer to me as 'the poet...' Michael Farley was the second published poet I met. They ran a poetry workshop for the Workers Educational Association in Leicester. I went when I was a student at Leicester Polytechnic. I told none of my friends. Poetry begins in secret.

[3] When I last spoke to Catherine, a few years ago, she had given up writing poetry and left England. She sent me a book, *Salmon: A Journey in Poetry, 1981-2007* as part of a dispersement of her library. So poetry is passed around. Michael Farley I lost track of many years ago – this was before social media – but occasionally I meet people who knew him. He was beautifully serious.

[4] From *The Passionate Measure,* Ivan V Lalić, translated by Francis R Jones, Anvil Press Poetry, 1989, and included in *Centres of Cataclysm,* edited by Sasha Dugdale, David Constantine & Helen Constantine, Modern Poetry in Translation/Bloodaxe Books, 2016.

[5] Or, 'Silent, upon a peak in Darien', as Keats suggested in his poem 'On First Looking Into Chapman's Homer'.

[6] Kanfanar is a small village in Croatia and lies at the interchange of the Istrian Y expressway/motorway B8 and A9, as well as on the Divača to Pula railway, and was formerly the junction of a branch-line to Rovinj, so I believe.

[7] Oh, and odd that 'lilac' should be an anagram (minus the accent on the 'c') of Lalić. Odd, irrelevant, but apt.

[8] Irina Ratushinskaya was released from a Soviet labour camp in late 1986 and the poetry she had written while in prison added to the mounting pressure on Mikhail Gorbachev to introduce Glasnost which led eventually to the end of the Soviet system.

[9] I was Literature Development Worker for South Humberside based in Scunthorpe, with Grimsby as the other jewel in my crown. I had a small budget and a telephone on a desk in Scunthorpe Central Library opposite Brigid, the Dance Development Worker, and with the Music Development Worker, Dan, always off somewhere banging cans and singing, and the Film Theatre just downstairs run by my dear, late friend Tony Whitehead, who loved *Carry On* films and Avant Garde French Cinema, and could tell the difference between the two.

[10] *Poems Before & After: Collected English Translations,* Bloodaxe Books, 2006.

[11] Although he was not overtly political, after the Prague Spring of 1968 Holub became a *non-person* in Czechoslovakia.

[12] A film released in 1986, directed by Claude Berri and adapted from the novel by Marcel Pagno.

[13] And so apparently ending the long line of the Soubeyran family.

CHAPTER 2

Ted Hughes on vinyl – Windgather Cottage Youth Hostel – Slogging up hills – William Dunlop, leading poet – Shuttling darts – The Communist Party of Great Britain – The New Golden Treasury of English Verse – The Jam – Shelley, Keats, Spenser & me – Dad finds Crow – The possibility of Myxomatosis – Under cover of fading light.

In 1978 I heard a record of Ted Hughes reading some of his poems. I hadn't heard a poet reading their own work before and I had no idea who Ted Hughes was.[14] I was thirteen when the needle dropped onto the vinyl and his soft northern cadences filled the room. It was the voice I heard, not the words. There was a quiet certainty. The accent was unforced. The silences were precise. This was poetry as spoken art, not to be explained or understood. The record wasn't mine and I heard it at someone else's house – a thoughtful grown-up thinking I might be interested. I didn't ask to borrow it and it didn't cross my mind to try to buy a copy for myself.[15] I think eventually I got hold of a copy of Hughes' collection *The Hawk in the Rain*, but the book and the recording didn't connect in my mind, although I can still remember his reading of 'Six Young Men' and I think I read the poem once or twice myself.[16] Hearing him reading was an end in itself. Curious. Unsettling.

I also remember Hughes reading his poem 'Wind',

particularly for the lines:

> This house has been far out at sea all night,
> The woods crashing through darkness, the booming hills.

The poem is full of the concrete made abstract. It had a nerve, a poet saying simply that this is how it is. It introduced to me the idea that the landscape we inhabited was something more than simply the place in which we happened to find ourselves. For a boy who had spent most weekends and holidays walking and cycling around the British Isles this was an important understanding.[17] It began to explain to me why slogging up all those hills in bottom gear with a gale blowing was more than just madness. The poem finishes by driving home the idea that even the underlying rock was alive:

> We watch the fire blazing,
> And feel the roots of the house move, but sit on,
> Seeing the window tremble to come in,
> Hearing the stones cry out under the horizons.

Here was an experience of the natural world that I had shared with Hughes. I had stayed at Windgather Cottage Youth Hostel[18] in the Peak District while on a cycling tour with my dad when I was thirteen. The name was apt. A storm had pulled at the slates that night as we few hostellers huddled round a fire and played Monopoly. I can't remember if I had heard the poem before that night or if I played it back in my memory later, but suddenly I was living – had already lived – the life of the poet. Next morning we set off south, the country fresh and windswept. For nearly forty years I've carried, entwined, that stormy night at Windgather Cottage and Hughes' reading of his poem 'Wind'.

Then another thing happened. While I don't remember Hughes' own poetry at school I do remember the anthology he'd edited, *Here Today,*[19] but only for the poem 'Landscape as Werewolf' by William Dunlop. Not many people remember William Dunlop (1936 – 2005), but he had two poems in *Here Today* and in the 1950s and 60s he was considered one of the UK's leading poets. He managed to miss out on publishing a collection early on in his career, although Oxford University Press and Victor Gollanzc Limited were interested. He may have forgotten about 'Landscape with Werewolf' when he moved to the United States in the early 1960s as it wasn't included in his first collection, *Caruso for the Children and Other Poems*, which was finally published in the late 90s.[20] And when, two years after his death, the publication of a *Selected Poems* was made possible by private subscription from friends and admirers, 'Landscape with Werewolf' wasn't included.[21] Dunlop had given up writing poetry in the late 1960s. Then, from the 1990s until his death, there was a burst of late creativity. He was probably completely unware of how his short poem for young people was making its own way in the world through various dog-eared copies of *Here Today.*

Landscape as Werewolf

by William Dunlop

Near here, the last grey wolf
In England was clubbed down. Still,
After two hundred years, the same pinched wind
Rakes through his cairn of bones

As he squats quiet, watching daylight seep
Away from the scarred granite, and its going drain
The hills' bare faces. Far below,
A tiny bus twists on its stringy path
And scuttles home around a darkening bend.

The fells contract, regroup in starker form;
Dusk tightens on them, as the wind gets up
And stretches hungrily: tensed at the nape,
The coarse heath bristles like a living pelt.

The sheep are all penned in. Down at the pub
They sing, and shuttle darts: the hostellers
Dubbin their heavy boots. Above the crags
The first stars prick their eyes and bide their time.

You can see why Hughes selected it. While it doesn't have the daring leaps of imagination of so many of Hughes' poems, every word and phrase is darkly perfect. To anthropomorphise the fells is not original but it is well done. The language is functional and sharp. I like the description 'and shuttle darts': insignificant but accurate and somehow more revealing than the more obvious 'playing' or 'throwing'. And the line, 'The first stars prick their eyes and bide their time', focuses the hope and menace underlying the poem. Here is poetry that achieves its purpose so well that beyond the obvious there is really nothing to say about it. Good poetry sometimes shuts us up.

Although the house I grew up in was full of books,[22] very few seemed to have been bought new and our small town certainly didn't have a bookshop.[23] It had a library but I don't ever remember borrowing poetry. Somehow or other we did have a few poetry books in the house. Most of these my mum had gathered as a young woman working in a bakery but with an ambition to write poetry.[24] There was some Wordsworth and Blake and the *Collected Poems* of Dylan Thomas. I read a few poems but didn't find much in these collections – too difficult or too boring for a fifteen year old. In 1980 I bought, presumably from our town's WH Smiths, a paperback of the *New Golden Treasury of English Verse*, edited by Edward Leeson but based on Palgrave's original selection. While I didn't read it from cover to cover, it was mine and I thought at the time that in compact form here was all I needed to read in order to become some kind of poet. The poems were in chronological order, beginning with Anonymous and ending with Ted Hughes.

In the summer of the same year The Jam, a style-conscious but independently-minded post-punk band from the suburban south, released an album called *Sound Affects*. They were a smart band (they wore suits but not city suits), this was a smart album (the cover was a pastiche of the BBC sound effects records of the previous two decades) and the title was clever. The sleeve of the album had this on it:

From *Mask of Anarchy*
by Percy Bysshe Shelley

Rise like Lions after slumber
In unvanquishable number
Shake your chains to earth like dew
Which in sleep had fallen on you –
Ye are many – they are few.

Let a vast assembly be,
and with great solemnity
Declare with measured words that ye
Are, as God made ye, free –

The old laws of England – they
Whose reverend heads with age are grey,
Children of a wiser day;
And whose solemn voice must be
Thine own echo – Liberty!

I asked my mum, when she was next off to Oxford to spend a day asking people which brand of cigarettes they preferred,[25] if she could get me more poetry by this poet called Shelley. For my 17th birthday in 1981 I was given *The Poems of Percy Bysshe Shelley.* I was slightly embarrassed by it being bound in fancy imitation tooled leather – I didn't want a book that drew attention to itself or was pretending to be more than it was, I just wanted the words. Over the years I read only a handful of Shelley's poems. 'Ode to a Skylark' and, at least once, the full 'Mask of Anarchy', but not the verse dramas 'Prometheus Unbound' or 'The Cenci'. His long elegy for John Keats, 'Adonaïs', I think I did read because I then took myself off to Oxford and bought *Keats Poetical Works* from Blackwell's Bookshop.

I knew a bit about Shelley and about Wordsworth and Coleridge and Byron, and I had had to read a bit of Chaucer and Pope for O-Level and A-Level English Literature respectively, and I didn't doubt the importance of any of them, but I read John Keats because I wanted to. For a while I thought I was Keats.[26] Here was a man often out of his depth – socially, academically, physically – but trusting everything to poetry. And while there are currents of complexity and subtlety awash in his work, even as a seventeen year old destined to possess only one A-Level I felt I was as capable of being affected by his poetry as any scholar. I hoped I was reading Keats, every line and every word, with the same appetite that Keats read Shakespeare or read Chapman's translations of Homer. The Jam had given me Shelley and Shelley had given me Keats and now Keats was my band. And because Keats admired Edmund Spenser I took the train to Oxford again and bought *Spenser's Poetical Works*, and in the summer of 1982, after failing my A-Levels and in theory looking for a job, I read 'The Faerie Queen'. While I didn't appreciate much of Spenser, there was hardly a poem of Keats that didn't in some way catch in my mind. Privately I made him my study.

The autumn after my summer with Spenser and Keats my dad found a pile of what looked like discarded English Literature textbooks and set-texts on the roadside as he was cycling home from work, including Hughes' collection *Crow*. We were used to Dad coming in with a saddle bag full of things he had hunted and gathered – blackberries, apples, sloes, rabbits, pigeons, even pheasants – the former being liberated from trees on both sides of the fence and the latter being roadkill. Waste not want not. Books we had not expected, but in they came and I was suddenly the owner of a battered, rain-stained, abandoned copy of *Crow*.[27] It seemed fitting that it came to me as a found book scavenged from the roadside. I read it, largely without understanding but aware that this was a different kind of poetry, certainly not Keats or even Hughes' early work. It was demanding stuff but not because of arcane language or syntax. It was precise in its opaqueness, seemingly rough and unpolished while carefully constructed and with a voice that was neither man nor beast. It stuck in my mind.

That my dad gave this haul of literary driftwood to me and not to my sister was because by our mid-teens it had been noted that I was the one reading poetry. At about this time Dad also gave me the slip-cased faux red leather-bound[28] collected works of Shakespeare that he had bought at some point in his early twenties. My mum was certainly a reader, had taken an A-level later on in life and had read poetry from being a young woman, but for my dad it was part of the discipline required by those who wanted the world to change. One of the things his membership of the Communist Party of Great Britain gave him was a faith in the value of reading for improvement and enlightenment. At the factory he read in whatever breaks there were and all through his dinner time. And he read when he got up for his breakfast alone at 5am every morning. The books came mostly from the library. I don't think he read for pleasure. Reading was part of the struggle and so reading should be a bit of a struggle. I know what he means.

Along with a house full of books we had plenty of records of classical music and some folk music and a recording of the Red Army Ensemble singing 'Songs from the Urals'. Classical music was like literature, it was ours to claim and claim it we should. Folk music was where dancing met the radical tradition, and male Davidsons love to dance.[29] It was from Russia because anything Russian was considered to have a melancholy grandeur as befitted the then leaders of the world's workers. I was the next in a line of working class people trying to hunt and gather what we hoped was high, improving culture, just as my Dad, as he cycled his twenty miles to the factory and back through the Oxfordshire countryside, would keep his eye out for late blackberries or a rabbit clipped by a car.[30] We knew there was good stuff out there and we believed it belonged to us, but we took it – including poetry – under the cover of fading light.

14 I didn't know that Ted Hughes had founded the magazine *Modern Poetry in Translation* with Daniel Weissbort in 1965 or that he had, in the process, published poems by Ivan V. Lalić.

15 At that age I owned precisely zero records.

16 *The Hawk in the Rain* by Ted Hughes, Faber, 1957.

17 Every year, from when I was eight, our holidays consisted of walking or cycling and staying at youth hostels, with the exception of the one year we took a package holiday courtesy of Progressive Tours, to spend a week on the Black Sea in Bulgaria. Keats would have enjoyed the trip to the collective farm: eat what you like from the trees and fruit bushes, they told us.

18 Which operated as a Youth Hostel from 1939 to 1983; it couldn't have been better named.

19 Hutchinson, 1963, with an introduction by Ted Hughes.

20 Rose Alley Press, Seattle, USA, 1997.

21 Classic Day Publishing, USA, 2007.

22 So many books, from the works of Marx & Engels to a book on Scottish tartans and one about sex called, *You've Got to Have Love.*

23 Didcot, since you ask. It had a railway junction, power station, canning factory, but no bookshop. The final instalment of a three volume history of Didcot by the town librarian, Brian Lingham, was called *Dreams and Delusions.* Not without reason do

we Didcotians excel in limited ambition.

24 In her early twenties, she had a poem published in *The Liverpool Echo*.

25 My mum had left the bakery and didn't like the succession of cleaning jobs she'd picked up, but it turned out she liked stopping people in the streets and asking them questions. A couple of years later a bloke she interviewed told her he ran the Oxford Playhouse. She asked if her son could come and ask him some questions about what arts administration might be. I did and it sounded better than being a wages clerk. So my life changed direction because the Chief Executive of the Oxford Playhouse smoked Benson & Hedges Silk Cut.

26 I also thought I was Jude Fawley from Thomas Hardy's *Jude the Obscure*, partly because I had been up on the Downs south of Didcot and looked north to the dreaming spires of Oxford (Hardy's Christchurch) and felt that I was an outsider looking in, as I was, and as I still am.

27 He'd found them on the roadside somewhere between Nuneham Courteney and Clifton Hampden on the little road that heads south and slightly downhill towards the bridge over the River Thames, which, as Spenser noted, runs 'softly till I end my song.'

28 Or it may be real leather but such fine leather that it looked faux.

29 The latest generation of Davidsons, male and female, all know how to cut a rug too.

30 That these rabbits may have been hit by cars because they had myxomatosis never crossed our minds. It was free food and no one died, until much later.

CHAPTER 3

'See, Master Proud-Face!' – Walter de la Mere – Basil Bunting on getting the sound right – 'Full Moon and Little Frieda' – A pin-stripe suit and a plastic bag – Jenny Joseph in a medieval setting – Sleeping peacefully – Silently reading with Roy Fisher – Silently reading with Ian McMillan – My mum and Walter de la Mare.

In the early 2000s I rescued from my parent's house – the only house I had ever known as a child – a book of poems. The date of publication suggests it was a feature in my life at age one or two. It is called *Poems*, written by Walter de la Mare, edited by Eleanor Graham, illustrated by Margery Gill, and published in 1962 by Penguin as a Puffin Book priced four shillings. The front cover is a gorgeous pen and ink illustration of a young girl enveloped by a bush of red roses. The book was aimed, I imagine, at parents or grandparents or doting uncles or aunts. It has the appearance of being precious but not exclusive. It is a product of that grand auto-didactic tradition that wanted to give books to everyone who wanted them regardless of their social or economic status. The poems were written to be read aloud. That is what happened in my case. My mum read the poems to me and I'm sure to my sister too, and read them again and again. And again. One page has been turned to so often that for most of its existence it has been held together by yellowing Sellotape. On the page opposite the text is a line drawing of a boy on his mother's lap. The poem is called 'Won't' and plays on a child's terrible petulance turned inside out in the final lines by his mother's love. Here it is:

Won't

by Walter de la Mare

See, Master Proud-Face!
Cold as a stone;
Light, life, love
From his bright eyes gone;
Pale as a pudding
His smooth round cheek;
His head like a block
On his still, wooden neck.

Won't, says his cherry mouth;
Won't, says his chin;
Won't, says the Spectre,
His bosom within;
Won't, says his clenched fist;
Won't, says his foot;
Every single inch of him
Shouts, I will *NOT!*....

Poor, poor Mamma –
She mopes in her room,
Pining and pining
For the moment to come
When her short sharp you *SHALL!*
She can safely unsay,
And the sun sparkle out,

And the tears dry away;

Yes, her whole heart is sighing
In passionate trust
For a kiss from those *Won'ts*
To make hay of her Must!

This poem is about me and my mum. That's obvious. How could Walter de la Mare have known? About us? About how we were? It's a mystery. I cannot guess now what thoughts I had about this poem fifty years ago, but my adult self is reminded that some poems *hear us* even while we are hearing them. I know that this poem *heard me* then and it still *hears me* now. I have read it many times since it resurfaced into my life twenty years ago and of course it is my mum's voice I hear, her slight Lancastrian accent, her concern to pronounce every word correctly, her pitch and moment, her apron smelling of cooking and the kitchen.

Even if I set aside the close personal relationship I have with this poem, I can see that it is a deftly constructed piece, composed rather than written. It is worth taking apart and re-assembling just to see how it works. It may look like a handful of words ranged down the page, but fifty years on every syllable still drops into the silence as sweetly as stones into a well. By hearing this poem – and probably others – I may have got some understanding of what makes a line of poetry hang in the air like a little kite. I don't think it would have had the same effect had I come across it when I was older and able to read to myself. I would have been reading not listening. I was, anyway, not good at reading and had been given special lessons in primary school.[31] Up until nine or ten I was keener on listening – and talking – than reading and writing.

The poet Basil Bunting recognised the importance of listening regardless of how highly regarded was the poem or the poet.[32] In an essay late in his career, he reminds us that the ears hear what the eyes can only dimly see (as well as offering a neat critique of the idea of prose poetry):

> Reading in silence is the source of half the misconceptions that have caused the public to distrust poetry. Without the sound, the reader looks at the lines as he looks at prose, seeking a meaning. Prose exists to convey meaning, and no meaning such as prose conveys can be expressed as well in poetry. That is not poetry's business.[33]

I'm tempted to quote the whole essay, because it is clear that he thinks of poetry as sound as well as sense, which is just as we first appreciate it as children and as we should try to appreciate it as adults. In the preface to his *Collected Poems* (1968) he says:

> I believe that the fundamental thing in poetry is the sound, so that, whatever the meaning may be, whatever your ultimate intention in that direction might be, if you haven't got the sound right, it isn't a poem.[34]

Getting sound right should be the first duty of the poet if they aspire to write *poetry* and not merely to write.

Ted Hughes got the sound right. I saw him read live only once. His reading – almost a recitation – was perfect and appeared effortless. There was no need to see him a second time, although I would happily have done so, as the impact was immediate and lasting. He walked onto the stage of a theatre in York, with not an empty seat in the house, dressed rather formally, a suit with perhaps a small pin-stripe and I feel sure he wore a tie. He had a bag, possibly even a plastic bag. From this he drew his sheaf of poems. His introductions were short. Other than the poem 'Full Moon and Little Frieda', I can't remember exactly which poems he read. What I can remember is his stillness, how he let the words do the work, how he placed the sounds into the silence. And what a silence. Here's the opening stanza of 'Full Moon and Little Frieda':

A cool small evening shrunk to a dog bark and the
clank of a bucket
And you listening.
A spider's web, tense for the dew's touch.
A pail lifted, still and brimming mirror
To tempt a first star to a tremor.

And then that wonderful middle line. What a nerve to repeat 'moon' thrice and with an exclamation mark each time:

'Moon!' you cry suddenly, 'Moon! Moon!'

Bunting would have approved. Hughes was a poet who performed his poetry but he was not a *performance poet*. He was not playing the part of poet. In a word – and it is a word that is important to me – he *released* the poems. The poets I like, really like rather than just admire, do this, they release their poems. They do not present themselves or their histories or their joys and disciplines, they do not set out their stall or display their garish feathers. They simply place the sounds into the silence.

Sometimes the poets whose poems sound right are not the ones who appear to particularly relish strutting upon the stage. Having a fine pair of lungs, a talent for self-aggrandising self-deprecation and the appropriate patter to keep those at the back awake does not mean there will be good sounds or even poetry. I could not have anticipated in the mid-1980s that a reading by the late Jenny Joseph would stay with me but I distinctly remember about twenty minutes into her reading realising that I was entirely absorbed by the experience. I don't believe she was a poet famous for her performances, and her poetry is mostly quietly liked but not held aloft. Her words were spoken into the quiet of the medieval building in which the Leicester Poetry Society chose to hold its poetry readings and the sounds worked. I was not bored, although I had often been bored by poets reading. I was not impatient for one poem to end and the next to start, as I had sometimes been, a sure sign that the introductions were better than the poems. I was having poetry read to me and it was an end in itself. And if my eyes closed, as they still so often do, it was only to hear the words more clearly.[35] I have a memory that she read this short poem:

Bonfire

by Jenny Joseph

An hour or two till dusk with the wind fallen
We lit the fire, collecting all the junk
That over the months had soddened into the corners.
We swept the yard of crumpled leaves and sweet papers
Dusty and rotting.

'That'll never catch, all that damp soggy stuff
And the stench will be awful.'

Suddenly there shot up a flame
Very bright and clear through the coiling rolls
Of oily smoke, and it seemed to burn up the smoke;
Bright, inimitable, worth it.

Then as unaccountably it died.

Ash is everywhere.
Now it is dark
And none of this black ruin will light again.[36]

The book it is from, *Rose in the Afternoon and other poems*, has a dark red cover, no illustration or image. It was nicely produced but keen not to draw attention to itself. I certainly read it later, though it isn't a book I return to. But I remember the poetry reading she gave.

In that instance I was having poems read *to me* but with the right conditions reading to oneself can be just as powerful, even when reading silently. In 2016 over a period of days I read the late Roy Fisher's complete poems, including this short unassuming lyric:[37]

Linear

by Roy Fisher

To travel and feel
the world growing old on your body

breathe and excrete
perpetually the erosion that makes the world

a caravan the little city
that has the wit to cross a continent

so patiently it cannot help but see
how each day's dust lay and shifted and lies again

no forgotten miles or kinks
in the journey other than cunning ones

to pass through many things acquisitively
and touch against many more

I did the same in that year with Ian McMillan's *New and Selected Poems*. This poem is from what I'm sure Ian will describe as his 'middle period':[38]

Platform 2
by Ian McMillan

We are both waiting and he comes over to me,
His cap is dark. *I found my dad*

He says, as though he knows me. *Good* I say,
That's good. His cap, his cap is dark.

At stair bottom Ian. He'd hung hissen.
His cap, his cap, his cap is dark.

He must have been low, Ian, to do that
Does tha think? His cap, his cap, his cap, his

Cap is dark. *I allus get a return ticket,*
Just in case. His cap, his cap, his cap, his cap

You know the rest

Both are poets whose speaking voice I knew well, but I wanted to hear their work uncoupled from the personality inherent in their voices. I wasn't alone so I read silently, reading their poems as they had been set out on the page and telling myself to take the sound and sense of each line before allowing the next line to present itself. After a while the poems float away from their creators and become just the words. It is a different pleasure to experience them in that way. And it is a different pleasure to read them without the urgency of reading prose. As Basil Bunting hinted at in the earlier quotation, it is surprisingly difficult to avoid reading poetry as we read prose, and yet poetry should not try to do what prose does, or there will be trouble.[39] Having trained ourselves to read quickly, having been encouraged to gobble up the pages because so many other pages are frying in the pan like noisy sausages, it is not easy to take each line of poetry as it comes. I blame books.

Two hundred years ago my people – possibly illiterate and certainly with little access to the printed word – would have been more likely to have heard, memorised and then spoken poetry aloud than to read it themselves. If they were literate they probably didn't own any books other than a Bible.[40] On my dad's side they were certainly working on farms or as sailors and then in factories. How would they have reacted to the sight of someone reading silently to themselves – not sounding the words out aloud, not sharing them? I think they would have been intrigued and impressed – although, equally, I suspect they would have pointed out that if only one book were to hand it would be nice to share it by reading aloud, Comrade Scholar! There is, for all its convenience, a selfishness about reading silently, as if the words are yours and yours alone. Perhaps this is why a small portion of the world still insists on reading poetry to each other, face to face. Whatever the quality of the poetry, it is at least being shared. We like to do things together, human beings.

So I return to the mum – or dad – reading poetry to the child, and to poetry as the sounds that carry best when everyone is breathing the same air in the same room. This is the Poetry Commonwealth, the sharing of poetry as if that was the reason for poetry. Not for private gain or private pleasure but for the people. The poem, 'Won't' was shared by Walter de la Mare with his readers and then my mum in turn shared it with me. She made a silence and in that silence offered me those sounds. As a child I demanded to hear it and I filled it out with what little sense of self I had. And I have made silences in my adult life to share it again. It is such a slight thing, I know, both the poem and the hearing of it, hardly significant. But from this poem – a good thing but not a work of genius – I took all I needed to know about sound and about sense and the transmission of thought and emotion and why it is important, somehow or other, to hear poetry.

[31] I was categorised in primary school as a remedial reader and because my handwriting was so terrible I wasn't keen on writing either.

[32] Basil Bunting sounds like he should be in a Walter de la Mare poem. Never can a serious modernist poet have had such a song-like and unprepossessing name.

[33] *The Poet's Point of View*, 1966, reprinted in *Briggflatts*, Bloodaxe Books, 2009.

[34] From the preface to *Collected Poems*, 1968, reprinted in *Briggflatts*, Bloodaxe Books, 2009. I don't do tattoos but if I did, I'd have that first sentence down my left calf, with a little bit extra on my foot – a footnote, I suppose – referencing its author.

[35] But actually, what greater pleasure is there than to be lulled to sleep by a poet reading their verse. The rise and fall of their voice puts our cares to flight and so we wake, several hours later, refreshed and happy.

[36] *Rose in the Afternoon and other poems*, J M Dent & Sons Ltd, 1974.

[37] From *The Long and the Short of It: Poems 1955 – 2010*, Bloodaxe Books, 2012.

[38] *To Fold the Evening Star: New & Selected Poems*, Carcanet, 2016.

[39] It is similar disputes about demarcation that arguably hobbled the British car industry in the 1980s, although I think it was actually lack of investment as capital had its bond with land and labour broken following Margaret Thatcher's relaxing of financial regulations.

[40] Although on my dad's side I come from an august line of atheist, socialist, republicans going back generations.

CHAPTER 4

Sonnet by a Midlander – How to read it – 'Dancing at Oakmead Road' by Maura Dooley – Line endings – W S Graham reads 'Lines on Roger Hilton's Watch' by W S Graham – Edwin Morgan reads 'Strawberries by Edwin Morgan – Mollie Davidson reads 'Meditation on the A30' by John Betjeman – What Hamlet said to the Players.

Here's Shakespeare's sonnet No. 116:

Let me not to the marriage of true minds
Admit impediments. Love is not love
Which alters when it alteration finds,
Or bends with the remover to remove.
O no! it is an ever-fixed mark
That looks on tempests and is never shaken;
It is the star to every wand'ring bark,
Whose worth's unknown, although his height be taken.
Love's not Time's fool, though rosy lips and cheeks
Within his bending sickle's compass come;
Love alters not with his brief hours and weeks,
But bears it out even to the edge of doom.
If this be error and upon me prov'd,
I never writ, nor no man ever lov'd.

It contains in its text instructions for a reader. The metre and the rhyme scheme are obvious and I can't believe Shakespeare wanted anyone reading the poem to fight against either of these aspects. The line-endings should also be acknowledged as they hold the metre in their frame. The punctuation, which was given when it was first published in 1609, unlocks the sense very nicely. The emotional weight of the poem lies in its final lines and here the clusters of consonants are demanding enough on the human mouth that they have to be read slowly. Lines that deliver themselves slowly have impact. Read quickly, or read with no regard for the metre or the rhyme scheme or the punctuation, and it becomes a much more difficult poem to appreciate. The ideas need to be played out as Shakespeare has suggested through all the poetic choices he has made in shaping the poem. It tells us how it should be said.[41]

Musical scores exist not only to record music for posterity and to allow a group of musicians to operate together but also so that you've got something to merchandise – a commodity that can be traded. And although sharing the basic notes might well be enough, composers clearly wanted to send out their music with other instructions to ensure it was played – and heard – in its best form. Playwrights have done the same, most famously Beckett with his instructions about how long pauses should be. While such advice can't stop bad performances – of plays or music or poetry – they give a space in which a performer can work. We want a piece of music to be a seamless thing, for us to be largely unaware of the mechanics of the piece, although we know there is stuff going on. And in poetry, although we don't want to hear the line-endings or rhyme scheme like a clash of cymbals,[42] anyone listening to a poem should be able to find the shape of the poem in the sound it makes.

Here is a poem that on paper emphasises its formality: metre, line-length/line-endings, and stanza form:

Dancing at Oakmead Road

by Maura Dooley

Sometimes I think of its bright cramped spaces,
the child who grew there and the one we lost,
how when we swept up for its newest lover
the empty rooms were still so full of us.

The honeyed boards I knew would yet hold close
our dusts, some silver from my father's head,
the resin of the wood would somehow catch
in patina the pattern of his tread.

That time in the back room, laughing and drunk,
Geraldo and his orchestra, a tune
that had you up and waltzing and me quiet,
my throat so achey at the sight of you,

glimpsing for a second how it might have been
before his mouth went down on yours, before
the War, before the children broke into
the dance, before the yoke of work. Before.

A few years ago I was listening to a recording of Maura Dooley reading this poem. I wanted to share the poem as part of a poetry reading. I had her permission but I didn't have the text to hand (I had lent the book to someone) and even the internet couldn't find it for me. What I could get was an audio recording of her reading the poem, so I transcribed the text from the recording and tried to write it out as I thought the reading suggested, with line-endings and stanza breaks intact. Her reading of the first section offered me the first stanza in all its measured formality, as if she paced the room and turned to mark the end of each line:

Sometimes I think of its bright cramped spaces,
the child who grew there and the one we lost,
how when we swept up for its newest lover
the empty rooms were still so full of us.

Perhaps the verse here is too easy on the ear and flows too sweetly despite its dark echo, but her reading confirmed that the poem needed this first stanza to allow a listener – or reader – to settle down and become attuned to her way of writing.

Her reading of what became the second stanza started to push at the structure slightly. The first two lines break the sense, or rather force a tiny pause which both makes it easier to speak and offers a little moment of revelation when we realise it is dust – not a living being – that is being held close:

The honeyed boards I knew would yet hold close
our dusts

And the fourth line of this stanza is held up for a moment by the word 'catch' in the previous line, allowing the wonderful music of movement to dance itself out:

would somehow catch
in patina the pattern of his tread.

Now we are expecting the stanza structure the sense of the poem can work against it. A good, subtle reading of the poem will suggest this intent while keeping it in check. The break between the penultimate and last stanza is used to great effect:

and me quiet,
my throat so achey at the sight of you,

glimpsing for a second how it might have been

I take this stanza break to be that feeling so accurately observed in the line before, the moment when a speaker thinks they might cry so holds off speaking for a second to gather their composure. So much is given through that slight pause demanded by the stanza break. The silence must be read and held to allow us to hear and feel dramatically what is being communicated.

The final stanza is a lesson in how an everyday word can be loaded with meaning through the simple – complex – act of throwing it in gentle arcs from one end of a stanza to the other, something that works because there is a stanza form present with all its controlling formality:

> before his mouth went down on yours, before
> the War, before the children broke into
> the dance, before the yoke of work. Before.

The line endings keep the rhyme of 'before' and 'War' from being too close. And after the word 'into' it is the line ending that forces us to pause as if the dance has itself been held up for a moment. The final 'before' is a perfectly understated final chord. It has to be read – it was read – with just the right balance between casual familiarity and dark finality. And of course to *finish* a poem with the word *before* is itself a small delight, turning on its head the usual approach to storytelling. Maura Dooley's reading of it and how I found myself writing it and as it was in fact published were all of a single purpose. Like Shakespeare's sonnet, it builds into its fabric the notation necessary to read it aloud and as it should be read aloud. And it should be read aloud. It is a very good poem.

Poems which appear much less formal are just as likely to contain instructions for their performance. W S Graham's elegy, 'Lines on Roger Hilton's Watch', appears to use line endings to make a fluent reading more difficult and there is a temptation to simply roll the lines together into what might be mistaken for prose.[43] But it is not prose. And if, for instance, its closing lines are read with respect it is the jaggedness of its sound that makes it glitter like granite:

Watch, it is time I wound
You up again. I am
Very much not your dear
Last master but we had
Terrible times together.

The recording of W S Graham reading this poem confirms that this is how the poet thought it should be read.[44] Even at points where the sense suggests the lines should run on, he gives a little pause and in most places the turning of the corner from line to line is pronounced. Presumably, Graham felt that these short, sharp lines were the very essence of the poem – why else would he have written in this form? In his reading it is possible to hear this important but subtle bass line being played out.[45]

Edwin Morgan's poem 'Strawberries' looks similar in form, short lines with line-breaks running across the sense, but again hearing a recording of him reading it confirms that line length is there for a reason. There is a certain drive, a certain breathlessness, a certain uncertainty communicated by breaking the flow of the text in this way, right up until the final, cinematic line:

let the sun beat
on our forgetfulness
one hour of all
the heat intense
and summer lightning
on the Kilpatrick hills

let the storm wash the plates

I have heard Edwin Morgan read this poem – live and on recordings – and I have heard other people read it. My daughter, Mollie, learned it by heart a few years ago as part of a national competition for poetry spoken from memory. Her speaking of the poem carried, to my paternal ear at least, just that necessary amount of anticipated joy, even though her life experience was very different from Morgan's. Or rather, she found some communality which is what the Poetry Commonwealth yields so freely. You do not have to be the poet to read the poem with understanding. The point of the poem is communication.

Years earlier, when Mollie was nine or ten I had bought a voice recorder and asked her – I was a demanding parent – to be recorded reading some well-known poems. The recordings are lost now. They were lovely to hear but also instructive. They were lovely because I heard a smart young person handle a collection of rather complex words. She did well, letting each poem lead and guide her reading. The words when clearly spoken offered the sense of each piece and the hesitations and revelations that come with a first reading gave a thrilling immediacy. My favourite was her reading of 'Meditation on the A30' by John Betjeman and the moment when Mollie realised she was going to have to read the word 'bastard'. There was a micro-pause as she worked through the implications of using a word her parents would have frowned upon, and then she plunged on, and rattled through the rest of the poem. Her delight and even excitement at realising how delightful and exciting a poem can be when the words become our own was a pleasure.

She had followed Shakespeare's advice, as given by Hamlet to his actors in Act III, Scene 2: 'Speak the speech, I pray you, as I pronounced it to you, trippingly on the tongue.' 'Trippingly' is a word we don't always associate with poetry readings, but if we interpret it as merely speaking with a regard to clarity of diction and the presence of metre then it has its place. Let the words do the work, Shakespeare is essentially telling us. If the poem needs sound effects, trap-doors, blackouts and unasked for curtain calls – to borrow a handful of theatrical devices – then perhaps the poem isn't up to scratch. Balance is all, he tells us: 'Suit the action to the word, the word to the action, with this special observance, that you o'erstep not the modesty of nature.' He knew his verse would work if it was read as it was written because at his best he was in complete control of his art. Any good poem will know how it wants to be read. Poems that aren't so good are all over the place.

41 And in doing so he also makes it rather easy to learn by heart.

42 Unless for comic effect, and then funnier still is the rhyme that is expected but doesn't arrive.

43 W S Graham (1918 – 1986).

44 Available on www.poetryarchive.org.

45 Poetry is more than the melody of sentiment, it needs a platform to base itself upon. Try mumbling a poem to hear what's really going on and why that base line is so important.

CHAPTER 5

Paul Durcan is seriously funny – 'Darling' by Jackie Kay – They weep openly in Corby – Michael Donaghy on his tight-rope – Reading with trainee chefs – Rattling pans – Pigeons with poems – We don't mind if it rains – It rains – Christopher Fox performs Kurt Schwitters – 'Fümms bö wö tää zää Uu' – Stop laughing at the back.

Paul Durcan is a self-less performer of his own poetry. The genius of his performance lies in being absolutely at one with the poem, not as a writer but as a speaker. Even read from the page, each poem becomes a drama in which Durcan casts himself in all parts, absurd sometimes but always convincing. His delivery has a conviction that dares the audience not to laugh, although eventually they have to. The comedy is that he is serious. And the more serious he is the funnier and more moving become his poems. There are no rambling pre-ambles and no conspiratorial asides. There is no discussion of craft or even much about the genesis of each poem. Just the poet and the poems. And some silence in which to work. In my experience of organising poetry readings with Paul Durcan his personal preparation was strangely important.[46] He needed a quiet place to compose himself, he needed some time to acclimatise. When he stepped on stage there was a sense of risk. It could all go, it seemed, very wrong, but it never did. And for all that his readings of his own poems are distinctive, they work very well in other people's voices. Performed by the poet a lot is gained, but well performed by others nothing is lost.

In Carol Ann Duffy's performances everything is held back except the poetry. She is not unapproachable, but like Durcan's performances, there is a sense that this is about the poetry not the personality. Her accent – not distinctly anything but distinctly not received pronunciation – places the words rather simply into the silence.[47] While her introductions are friendly and informative and useful, they are not part of the poems. The poems have to look after themselves, which they are more than capable of doing. Jackie Kay's poetry readings are more closely intertwined with her personality. Her poems are perhaps no more autobiographical than many of Durcan's or Duffy's, but she reveals the poems as coming directly from her experiences. Her poem, 'Darling', written after the death of her friend the poet Julia Darling, does not need any introduction but becomes more powerful, of course, when the personal connection is explained.[48]

Darling

by Jackie Kay

You might forget the exact sound of her voice
Or how her face looked when sleeping.
You might forget the sound of her quiet weeping
Curled into the shape of a half moon,

When smaller than her self, she seemed already to be leaving
Before she left, when the blossom was on the trees
And the sun was out, and all seemed good in the world.
I held her hand and sang a song from when I was a girl –

Heil Ya Ho Boys, Let her go Boys
And when I stopped singing she had slipped away,
Already a slip of a girl again, skipping off,
Her heart light, her face almost smiling.

And what I didn't know or couldn't see then
Was that she hadn't really gone.
The dead don't go till you do, loved ones.
The dead are still here holding our hands.[49]

I mention these three poets – Durcan, Duffy and Kay – because I have heard them perform many times over several decades and often enough to appreciate the particular artistry they bring to a very challenging environment. Poetry audiences don't applaud every silence and plenty of poems are not funny enough for laughter. For the poet performing the response is the particular quality of silence that comes with concentration. Audiences are there to listen rather than sing along,[50] which shouldn't make the experience any less rewarding or any less communal. Poets have to perform not simply to get the response of the audience but to offer the poem so that the audience can make of it what they will.

In some locations there's an unexpected poetry. At a reading in the ex-steel making town of Corby in Northamptonshire – a town that in the 1950s had become home to thousands of Scottish families – Liz Lochhead brought herself and her audience to tears with these lines towards the end of her deceptively simple poem called 'After the War':[51]

All the unmarried uncles were restless,
champing at the bit
for New Zealand, The Black Country, Corby.
My aunties saved up for the New Look.

As she named their town there was a sudden charge of electricity in the room. She stopped reading. She was, for a moment, caught out by the memories the poem references. After a pause she carried on. For those seconds the audience had found themselves within the poem. Liz Lochhead's personal history stood for their collective history, with all the particular loss and disappointment of working class life that doesn't normally make it to the big screen, as it were. At that moment the poetry meant something. It was a transaction of incalculable value. It was communication.

The late Michael Donaghy could create equally powerful moments in the performance of his poems, although he didn't rely on chance. Learning many of his poems by heart, he was able, despite their complexity, to perform them as if they had just now come to mind. His means of connecting with the audience was simply to look directly at them as he spoke and to in effect ask them to be complicit in the risk of performing poetry without the safety net of a book to hand. It was impossible not to concentrate. It was impossible not to be with him as he stepped out above us on his tightrope of words. And for the poet Rita Dove, a US Poet Laureate, her brilliance was to step onto a stage in Birmingham (UK) as if her three thousand mile flight from West Virginia had been a couple of stops on the Midland Metro. The poetry world became smaller and more hospitable as she thanked *us* for making the effort to be with her. Sometimes all that is needed for communication to happen is for a poet to have made a journey.

Even very good poets can't always compensate for the wrong environment. At a poetry reading I organised many years ago with Ian Duhig and Simon Armitage it turned out that the well-appointed room in the local college was adjacent to the college kitchens, that evening being used by the catering course to prepare a sumptuous feast to impress their tutors and friends and family. Who would have thought that so much industrial language would be required during that process and that every saucepan – really, every saucepan – would need to be beaten with ladles on a regular basis? By an hour into the reading I was begging them, virtually down on my knees, to please for goodness sake, for the sake of poetry, cook a little more quietly.[52] The poetry was very good indeed, the evening for me was nothing but misery.

And what possessed me to put poets in shopping centres and on railway stations and in the foyers of multi-screen cinemas on a Saturday night? There is always a good reason but it gets lost, just as the poets sometimes do.[53] What didn't get lost were the racing pigeons who flew from the Shropshire village of Highley with tiny poems tied to their little legs. They clattered out of their baskets and circled several times to acquaint themselves with the lie of the land or the pull of magnetic north and then they were off, dashing back to their gaily painted pigeon loft in Digbeth carrying their precious cargo.[54] The human poets had watched with undisguised envy, then clambered back into the mini-bus to be taken to an important location, there to perform poems as part of a circumnavigation of the West Midlands bringing poetry to people who hadn't really asked for it.[55]

Poets *en plein air* is always a high risk strategy. In and out of the rain we ran from the third floor out-door terrace of the Library of Birmingham that unseasonably cold and inclement afternoon until the audience would move no more and said they would be pleased to get wet if they could only just listen to the poets. So listen they did. It is easy to underestimate a poetry audience's capacity for simply enjoying hearing poetry. The noise of the city around us, the street drummer plying his or her trade, the inevitable ambulances and fire engines and police cars, aircraft taking off from Birmingham International Airport are all frustrating distractions but they force an audience to concentrate. Sometimes we like things to be difficult. Sometimes art has to fight its corner and be seen to be punching above its weight. The pervasive, diurnal, immutable low-level misery of human existence is no match for a poem read with conviction, beneath an umbrella, in the drizzle of an English summer.

Kurt Schwitter's book-length sound poem *Ursonate* is as far away from the well-made poem as it is possible to be and makes huge demands on audiences. To the untrained ear it is a collection of grunts and squeaks, of snatches of the human voice speaking what might be German. To the ear that allows itself to listen it *is* a collection of grunts and squeaks, of course, but also a beguiling montage that allows the meaninglessness of modern life to become meaningful. The composer Christopher Fox is one of the few people in the UK capable of performing it. He uses a musical score and treats the piece as music, however broken it might sound. Last time I arranged for him to perform *Ursonate* we projected a giant photo of Kurt Schwitters to look down kindly from the back wall on our endeavours. Beaming, he was. That was a communal experience.[56] The opening lines are:

> Fümms bö wö tää zää Uu,
> pögiff,
> kwii Ee.

As Fox began performing a few in the audience looked at their friends and thought about laughing. Fox took no notice. He ploughed on, utterly absorbed in the shock and pleasure of performance. Schwitters smiled down on us from above. Amusement at such strangeness became concentration and a growing sense of understanding and then after forty minutes un-ironic utterly committed applause.

That performance was none the worse for the absence of Kurt Schwitters. Whether it was authentic or not is not easy to say and actually irrelevant. There are recordings of Schwitters performing *Ursonate* but their originality is questionable. Generations have gone by and Christopher Fox has inherited a tradition of performance as a composer and musician which is influenced by Schwitters but is not trying to recreate him or his time. The text remains the same and quite possibly the audience's initial incomprehension has carried across the decades. Others will carry the work into the future, as others will carry the work of many other poets into the future. The scores, as it were, are all freely available and, subject to permission, can be taken by anyone who cares to offer some other people the opportunity to listen. Period instruments are not required. Sprung dance floors are unnecessary. A gallery space with lovely light would be nice but can be dispensed with. There are no rules other than we continue to find something that passes for silence into which the poems can be placed.

46 I've not organised very many readings by Paul Durcan, and none recently, but I liked the that fact that he wanted to know about the audience, who they might be, if they would be familiar with his work, were there poems I thought he might particularly read.

47 Carol Ann Duffy's accent is hard to place. Born in Glasgow, she grew up in Staffordshire and that's not an accent that's easy to identify. I rather like the fact that her speech places her in England but doesn't name her region.

48 The text asks us to sing the first line of the third stanza. Two minutes on the internet will reveal the tune.

49 From *Darling: New & Selected Poems*, Bloodaxe, 2007.

50 Sadly, poetry karaoke has not caught on. Nor, for that matter, poetry tribute bands. There's a gap in the market.

51 From *A Choosing: Selected Poems*, Polygon, 2011.

52 And did their language need to be quite so *Gordon Ramsey*, for fuck's sake?

53 There's a good PhD to be written on poets getting lost. Or on poets arriving early (Ian McMillan being our leading early-arrivalist, although they do say that Dave Sheasby once arrived a year early for a reading). Or on poets not being able to drive.

54 This circling is known as kitting, something racing pigeons will do if they are just let out of their lofts to stretch their wings.

55 The important location was outside the Odeon cinema, Telford. The occasion was as part of the Cultural Olympiad in 2012. We resorted to using a megaphone.

56 In the Ikon gallery, Birmingham, as part of the Birmingham Literature Festival in 2012.

CHAPTER 6

A bloke with a German name – Another pin-stripe suit – Actors being directed – Making poetry-theatre shows – Leaving at half-time – What Helen Cross says – 'Begin again' with Brendan Kennelly – This needs a cello – 'Romantic Moment' with Tony Hoagland – Philip Larkin as he should be heard, with a Birmingham accent.

In 1984 or 1985 I went to a performance in the small studio theatre in The Leicester Haymarket Theatre. A man with a foreign-sounding name, who I now know was Ekkehard Schall, was performing his father-in-law's poems. He performed them in German. We had an English translation to read as the performance went on. There may have been a few songs. I think there was a piano on stage but I don't remember it being played. What I do remember was his pin-stripe suit and his hat with the silk hat band.[57] He was dapper and menacing but also ordinary and possibly a little overweight. I remember how he stalked about the stage and how he looked us in the eye, acknowledging that we were the audience for the poems. These he had by heart. It made a difference. His focus was on the words and their transmission to the audience, not on a script or a book. It was flattering. We were part of the performance. And while he recited the poems we glanced quickly at the translation, not wanting to take our eyes off him but wanting to know what he was going on about. It was difficult. I don't remember the poems he read, although it is likely that I have since come across some of them. What got me was his offering of the poems as important ideas. And his interest in us, the audience. And that it was a performance, not a reading. And that it was an artistic experience. His father-in-law was Bertolt Brecht.[58]

At that time, in the early 1980s, the standard opinion amongst my elders and betters in the poetry world was that actors ruined poetry. Looking back that seems a rather odd assertion, given that historically a number of important poets had been involved in the theatre and that Shakespeare was an actor and not a bad poet. I came out of Schall's performance thinking that an actor could be a really fantastic performer of poetry. Why had no one mentioned that to me before? Clearly a bit of effort needed to be applied and there were probably ways that a poem should *not* be performed – by an actor or a poet – but someone who knew what he or she was about could actually make poetry really rather good to listen to. As Schall through Brecht had demonstrated, there was another way of performing poetry, somewhere between the full-blown theatrical staging of a poem – as if it were a script, as if there were characters – and the leaden droning of a poem as if the performance and even the poem were of no value.

Schall was not *being* Brecht nor was he acting-out the story of the poems. He shared some physical characteristics with Brecht – his country of origin, his intonation, quite possibly his accent and perhaps his demeanour – but Schall was his own man. The Brecht poems were in many voices – some had been originally spoken by characters from his plays – but there was no changing of accent or even of hats. It was not necessary to act the poems. The words would do the work. He was, I realised many years later, simply releasing the poems through his body. Not as an actor but as a performer. That's a subtle difference. But whether actor or performer, he had been given direction with regard to his performance. He may have directed himself – he was well qualified to do so – or perhaps his wife, Barbara, had directed him. I'd like to think that old man Brecht himself had at some point stepped on stage in front of the boy Schall and recited one of his poems as if he brought truth to the masses, as if the future of the world depended on it, as if he wanted to be heard, as if he wanted to be understood.

For actors or performers to perform poems they *must* be directed. This is obvious.[59] But typically, when a decision has been made by an impresario to use an actor to speak poems he or she is chosen because those outside the profession think actors have good voices, can stand on stage without sweating and sometimes look younger than they are. Or older. Either way, the naïve organiser of the 'gala poetry reading' thinks it would be good to have an actor read some poems because they will read so nicely. And good actors are cheaper than good poets. And this one is from off the telly. This misses the point, which is that performers are trained to work for weeks or months or even years with complicated text – and even a good honest poem is an intricate piece of machinery at work in its various dimensions. Performers are trained to work with directors and often with many others – movement coaches, voice coaches, fight arrangers, set designers, etc. – in order to arrive at the moment of effortless performance. Just as we would not expect a poet to stand on stage and actually write poetry, so we shouldn't expect an actor to simply enter stage left and recite a poem. The performer may well sound nice but they will only be speaking the words.

Faced with a block of text but with none of the familiar layout or stage direction and with no one to assist them, the actor searches for whatever signs they can find indicating how to perform the poem. They will toy with accents, particularly if there are suggestions that the poet might come from a place where an accent that isn't received pronunciation might be dominant. They will make the understandable mistake of thinking all poems are autobiographical. Then they will look for narrative within the poem, allowing them at least to tell a story. Again, this is understandable as most plays are stories and some poems are as well. Finally, they will look for images that can be referenced or actions that can be mimicked. We might smirk at the sight of the actor blowing their frozen fingers energetically at the start of Keats' 'St Agnes' Eve' ('... ah, bitter chill it was, / the owl for all his feathers was a cold / and the hare limped trembling through the frozen grass') but it is quite reasonable that a performer should take this line as a piece of stage direction. With no other instruction, they are at least trying to find a way to present the poem. A thoughtful director will tell them that with good poetry you need to understand the poem and then let the words do the work.

Schall speaking Brecht's poems inspired me, fifteen years later, to produce what I called poetry-theatre productions. These used performers, a director, a composer and designers, all the resources of the performing arts, in the hope of giving to audiences quickly the pleasure to be had from some of the best contemporary poetry.[60] I started by acquiring the rights. That debt needed to be paid up-front. Then performers were hired and a director and a set designer and a sound designer who was also a composer and an assistant producer and someone to do PR and marketing. There was a lot of money invested, to be honest. Funding from Arts Council England and from box office income or fees from venues helped make this possible but there was still a financial risk. My friend, the novelist Helen Cross, says that at some point all writers have to engage with a market and I extend that idea to include poetry and its performance. This engaging with a market isn't necessarily about money. Disposable time is just as hard a currency to come by as cash, but either way people have to be persuaded to give what little time or money they have to an arts experience that has potentially no value. That's where the risk lies for all parties.

While the Brecht performance planted the seed, this adventure in performance had been inspired by the growing frustration I felt over a thirty year period with the quality of poetry readings as an artistic experience. The question I would ask myself as I took my seat at a poetry reading was could I invite a friend or neighbour to come along and feel confident that that friendship or neighbourliness would last the reading? So often, having extended the invitation, my companion could see that something of value was involved, and they were impressed by the books the poet had had published, and they respected the reverence that the poets garnered from the audience, but the reading of the poems often left them wishing they were elsewhere or thinking that they just couldn't understand poetry and it was all their fault and that they were not worthy. This made me angry because I knew in the world of theatre, or almost any of the performing arts, while the witless very often wasted the time of the feckless, the culture of departing at half-time in droves was equally strong.[61] Audiences for theatre were less easily cowed and more likely to have their own strongly held views about to what they would give their hard earned time. These audiences were also more likely *not* to be theatre practitioners themselves, so had nothing invested in the event other than a desire for an interesting evening.

Knowing that Bloodaxe Books shared my interest in broadening the audience for poetry I worked with their series of anthologies, beginning with *Staying Alive*.[62] With so many to choose from the forty poems we selected would all be exceptionally good. But with forty poets featured it would be impossible to involve all of them in person. The solution, obviously – and I confess this was my plan all along – was to work with three performers and to share the performing of the poems amongst them and to ask them – tell them, force them, command them

– to start by learning the poems by heart. Being trained actors they expected to do nothing less. They learn lines as part of their living. They are good at it. What followed was two very intense weeks of development and rehearsal during which, along with the creative team, the performers discovered how the poems might work. The challenge was made sharper by our commitment to not changing a single word of any poem and adding not one word either, not even by way of saying good evening or giving an introduction. In the first show, *Staying Alive,* and in subsequent productions, some poems may have been over-worked, perhaps too much theatricality applied or a line or two delivered with no regard to the metre, but the reaction from audiences was good. Some were surprised that poetry could be so easily enjoyed and so immediately understood.[63]

There was resistance. Over the years a couple of poets refused permission for their poems to be used.[64] Some literature festivals would have no truck with a production featuring poems but not the poets who wrote them. I suspect they may have been being loyal to poets who struggled to get opportunities to read aloud. Sometimes some of the audience felt that working so hard to make the poems enjoyable to listen to was betraying the nature of poetry, an art form that rightly demanded many years' investment in order to be understood. Sometimes they wondered if the poet themselves wouldn't have given a better performance. We stuck to our guns. The poets would be paid to write the work and stay at home and let's see what the world of the performing arts could do, for a change.

Brendan Kennelly's poem 'Begin' was used to close the first production, *Staying Alive.* It is a very fine poem that asks to be spoken aloud (and learned by heart).

Begin

by Brendan Kennelly

Begin again to the summoning birds
to the sight of the light at the window,
begin to the roar of morning traffic
all along Pembroke Road.
Every beginning is a promise
born in light and dying in dark
determination and exaltation of springtime
flowering the way to work.
Begin to the pageant of queuing girls
the arrogant loneliness of swans in the canal
bridges linking the past and future
old friends passing though with us still.
Begin to the loneliness that cannot end
since it perhaps is what makes us begin,
begin to wonder at unknown faces
at crying birds in the sudden rain
at branches stark in the willing sunlight
at seagulls foraging for bread
at couples sharing a sunny secret
alone together while making good.
Though we live in a world that dreams of ending
that always seems about to give in
something that will not acknowledge conclusion
insists that we forever begin.

We set this poem against a live cello performing a melodic sequence that repeated itself softly and then loudly, forcing the three performers who carried the text to rise against the tide of the music. Although a highly stylised performance – with the cello adding a fourth voice to the ensemble – it seemed to unleash the energy of the poem. And coming at the end of that performance, it was a call to the audience to leave the auditorium and begin again to read poetry. It was memorable and virtuosic.

Kennelly is a great performer of his own poetry and perhaps he writes poems that know how to be heard. Over the course of the six productions I made we also used many poems by American poets. Their poems often appeared effortless, loose-limbed and good to be around. Billy Collins, Rita Dove, Robert Hass, seemed to be able to consider complicated ideas with a language that was simple and direct and available to anyone. As Tony Hoagland shows in this poem, which we used from the *Being Human* anthology, the art is to disguise the art.

Romantic Moment

by Tony Hoagland

After seeing the nature documentary we walk
down Canyon Road,
onto the plaza of art galleries and high end clothing stores

where the orange trees are fragrant in the summer night
and the smooth adobe walls glow fleshlike in the dark.

It is just our second date, and we sit down on a bench,
holding hands, not looking at each other,

and if I were a peacock I'd flex my gluteal muscles to
erect and spread the quills of my Cinemax tail.

If she were a female walkingstick bug she might
insert her hypodermic probiscus delicately into my neck

and inject me with a rich hormonal sedative
before attaching her egg sac to my thoracic undercarriage,

and if I were a young chimpanzee I would break off
a nearby tree limb
and smash all the windows in the plaza jewelry stores.

And if she was a Brazilian leopard frog she would
wrap her impressive
tongue three times around my right thigh and

pummel me lightly against the surface of our pond
and I would know her feelings were sincere.

Instead we sit awhile in silence, until
she remarks that in the relative context of tortoises
and iguanas,

human males seem to be actually rather expressive.
And I say that female crocodiles really don't receive

enough credit for their gentleness.
Then she suggests that it is time for us to go

do something personal, hidden, and human.[65]

The poem takes a surprising turn, given its title, but it builds through very precise images to deliver something thought provoking. It is funny. And when spoken in a theatre space to an audience who are waiting for permission to laugh, that means it is laugh-out-loud funny, a comedy coming from the words not an actor.

Philip Larkin's poem, 'The Mower', from his *Collected Poems*, was also surprisingly good to hear.[66] For all that Larkin was not particularly known as an end-of-the-pier-show man, he knew how to master the moment. 'The Mower' was used in the production *Being Human,* and we drew more from it through our man Barrett Robertson using the sweetest of Birmingham accents. The poem didn't need Larkin's clipped vowels, it transpired, and the richness and pathos inherent in a West Midland's accent served the poem well.[67] Jackie Kay's poem 'Darling' was spoken by the other male performer in our *Being Human* production, Benedict Hastings,[68] and he gave the poem flight without any background information or personal connection with it. As audiences reminded us, sadly we are all acquainted with cancer.

Audiences said good things about the performers, and about the set and the music and the lighting, but most importantly they said they loved the poetry. The poetry – most of it new to most of the audience – had been given back to them and at the end of each performance it was the poems and the poets they applauded. There *was* an appetite for poetry if only poetry could present itself as if it wanted to be understood rather than admired. People said they normally couldn't *get* poetry and that they couldn't quite understand why as they liked films with sub-titles and read novels and looked at contemporary art. What Ekkhard Schall had demonstrated in 1984 was still true – the best poetry can be carried into the world by any number of different voices, that words are made to be spoken and heard, that a poem performed is an artistic experience that can be enjoyed by virtually anyone. And that rehearsals are a good idea, too.

57 Not dissimilar to that worn by Ted Hughes (in Chapter 3.). But not, I think, the same suit. Or was it?

58 Ekkehard Schall (1930 – 2005) was married to Brecht's daughter, Barbara. But you knew that.

[59] Anyone who simply gives an actor a poem and shoves them on stage to read is not serving the cause.

[60] Within my price range, and believe me, prices vary. Sadly the mechanism that prices airline flights on a day to day basis is not available to fix the price of poetry. Or perhaps not sadly.

[61] It is no surprise that much 'challenging theatre' dispenses with an interval. The desire for secondary spend at the ice-cream counter is no match for the fear that the punters might call it a day. And the mark-up on tubs is significant for your hard-pressed regional theatre. On Magnums less so.

[62] Bloodaxe Books, 2002.

[63] At least one attender regretted that he had been unable to enjoy the two hours of blissful slumber, as he had anticipated, because the poetry was so well delivered.

[64] Fair enough. Probably holding out for Hollywood. Their loss.

[65] From *Unincorporated Persons in the Late Honda Dynasty*, Graywolf Press/Bloodaxe Books, 2010.

[66] From *Collected Poems*, Ed. Anthony Thwaite, Faber, 1990.

[67] Not everyone agreed. Some people hated the idea that Larkin's words might be spoken with what was perceived as a working class accent, the rationale being that no one with such an accent could believably have such fine thoughts. I reach for my service revolver.

[68] Our third performer was Elinor Middleton and the Director was Steve Byrne.

CHAPTER 7

A dog called Scruff or Billy – 'The Barn' by Peter Didsbury – Jo Bell is 'Lifted' – Lock-wheeling with a windlass – Carol Ann Duffy's Prayer – An old maxim about sonnets – More bees in 'The Honeycomb' by Pauline Stainer – Stanley Cook and the Battle of Towton – 'Saddest' and 'Killing' – Gregory Leadbetter's dad tries to draw a horse.

I have been reading Peter Didsbury's poem 'The Barn' for thirty years. It is from his second collection, *The Classical Farm*, which I bought from an independent bookshop in Leicester.[69] The cover featured a small raggedly-looking dog – the sort of dog who'd be called Scruff or Billy – wearing a pair of deely boppers and sat on a cobbled street.[70] Everything about that cover said incongruity. What was this dog supposed to be doing, wearing such cheap and silly headgear? And did the cobbles reference an older England, probably northern? And what did *The Classical Farm* mean as a title and how did it relate to the image? The book was not a typical format but broader than usual, a shape chosen to carry Didsbury's longer than typical lines which also made best use of the cover picture. The format gave the poems a certain space on the page which reflected the space Didsbury gave himself in the poems, space to write with seemingly little regard for what anyone else was writing, to write with elegantly constructed sentences that seemed to reference the literary life of the 18th century rather than the 20th.

Unusually for me, for the first twenty years of my life with Didsbury's poem 'The Barn' I experienced it only on the page. It was a literary thing only. Later I heard Didsbury reciting the poem and now he can be heard reading it on The Poetry Archive. It is short but not to the point. It is a poem that seems to place itself in at least two time periods. There is a suggestion of it being inspired by a picture, although I couldn't say which. There is a suggestion also, to my ear, of the language of the *King James Bible,* although I couldn't say why. It plays with us.

The Barn

by Peter Didsbury

I stopped in the barn's wide entrance
where the dust and chaff were like bees.
With the light behind me, and my rake across my shoulder,
I knew I resembled The Harvest as often portrayed.

'Bees' is what we used to call
all kinds of insects then,
and bees were in my mind as I crossed
the floor to where he'd fallen.

I'd never known him dead before
and therefore did not see him straightaway
but thought he was a sack,
with barrow standing nearby ready to move him.

And move him I did,
though first I stood on that earthen floor
for a hundred years, while the language changed around me.

Dust. Chaff. The names of common things.
My hand moving up to touch my tightening cheeks,
to pick the pieces of broken bees from them.

That opening stanza is simple enough. If it were a chess game it would be one of the classic openings and as a poem it has a familiarity. It is nodding to the past and to a culture that brought forth great paintings with titles with Biblical resonance. The second stanza offers a charming distraction, a beautiful plot device as it transpires, and one that reminds us of the changing nature of language. This may be useful as we go on. We must have faith. The third stanza is a brilliantly fashioned axis around which the poem revolves. It is worth repeating:

I'd never known him dead before
and therefore did not see him straightaway
but thought he was a sack,
with barrow standing nearby ready to move him.

I find fascinating the feeling that we are looking through the crack of a door at a scene that compresses and distorts time. It is the opposite of a poem of instruction and although it is perfectly formed it does not offer neat ideas. The final stanza throws everything into confusion. Who are you, first person narrator? What relationship do we readers or listeners have with you? Is this about language or history or the culture of the countryside? And your 'tightening cheeks', is that age and death creeping up on you? And the 'pieces of broken bees'? What are they? What do they mean? I have thought about this poem often, inspired by the simplicity of its small explosion of possibility.

I met the poem 'Lifted' by Jo Bell in the early 2010s, initially through hearing it at readings and then in her collection *Kith*.[71]

Lifted

By Jo Bell

The land says – come uphill: and water says
I will. But take it slow.

A workman's ask and nothing fancy –
Will you? Here's an answer, engineered.

A leisurely machine, a box of oak and stone;
the mitred lock, the water's *YES*.

We're stopped. The bow bumps softly
at the bottom gate, and drifts.

All water wants, all water ever wants,
is to fall. So, we use the fall to lift us,

make of water its own tool, as simple
as a crowbar or a well-tied knot;

open up the paddles, let it dam and pucker,
swell and with it, lift us like a bride, a kite,

a wanted answer, breath no longer held
or like a boat. We're on our way

and rising. Water rushes in like fools;
these tonnages that slip across the cill,

all dirty-bottle green and gathering,
the torrent rushing to release itself, a giddy hurl

then slower, slow until it ends in glassy bulges,
hints of aftermath: a cool and thorough spending.

Wait, then, for the shudder in the gate,
the backward-drifting boat that tells you

there and here are level, an imbalance
righted. Ask of it – water; *help me rise*

and water says: *I will.*

It has a pleasing functionality, a simplicity about it, right from the start:

The land says – *come uphill*: and water says
I will. But take it slow.

It is honest about its intention which is simply to explain a piece of transport engineering:

All water wants, all water ever wants,
is to fall. So, we use that fall to lift us.

It is an explanation played out carefully over thirteen and a half couplets, the whole poem using a sense of balance to communicate the graceful transfer of energy that is the nature of the operation of a lock-gate on our canal system.[72] I think it is also about how we might live our lives, about love and sex, about the balance, the give and take, the risk inherent in our daily transfer of emotional energy.

Wait, then, for the shudder in the gate,
the backward-drifting boat that tells you

there and here are equal, an imbalance
righted. Ask of water; *help me rise*

and water says: *I will.*

For this reason alone – having the nerve to make a description of this piece of the industrial revolution into a meditation on being human – I admire it. Unlike 'The Barn', it is not laden with questions. Sometimes we want the certainty of stone and wood and water, of physics and engineering, especially when used as a metaphor for our heart's (dis-)content. It is also witty and moderately self-deprecating, the language ringing clear as water dropping off a windlass and every word fitted in place to make it possible to rise and fall along the canal system. It is a good, honest poem. Some of our friendships need to be this, with those in whose company we take a simple pleasure. The people we travel well with.

I can't remember how I fell in love with Carol Ann Duffy's poem 'Prayer', but love it I do.[73] It is the closing poem in her 1993 collection *Mean Time*[74] which I read on publication but it was possibly a decade later that, to paraphrase the poem, it *entered my heart.* I fell in love with it because I tried to learn it by heart.

Prayer
by Carol Ann Duffy

Some days, although we cannot pray, a prayer
utters itself. So, a woman will lift
her head from the sieve of her hands and stare
at the minims sung by a tree, a sudden gift.

Some nights, although we are faithless, the truth
enters our hearts, that small familiar pain;
then a man will stand stock-still, hearing his youth
in the distant Latin chanting of a train.

Pray for us now. Grade 1 piano scales
console the lodger looking out across
a Midlands town. Then dusk, and someone calls
a child's name as though they named their loss.

Darkness outside. Inside, the radio's prayer –
Rockall. Malin. Dogger. Finisterre.

It is a sonnet, which helps. The sonnet as a form is an example of the maxim that the greater the effort the poet expends in composing the poem the greater the ease with which the poem can be learned by heart.[75] There are more memorable forms – a succession of couplets, the ballad form, the limerick – but the sonnet in any of its versions gives itself to the memory with just the right amount of difficulty. It has such power because it is tightly bound. In a good sonnet not a word more is needed and not a word can be lost. It becomes memorable and it asks to be remembered. 'Prayer' is a poem that, like the *Lord's Prayer* and other bits of religious verse, wants to be learned. I still know it now, roughly. I revisit it regularly but not frequently, and like 'Lifted' its craft never fails to please. It is another good, honest poem that by using everyday materials and simple tools offers an imaginative response to our daily lives. I've no doubt I will be muttering it to myself at the end.

I have not learned 'The Honeycomb' by Pauline Stainer by heart and I don't read it very often, but the impression it made upon me so many years ago remains.

The Honeycomb

by Pauline Stainer

They had made love early in the high bed,
Not knowing the honeycomb stretched
Between lath and plaster of the outer wall.

For a century
The bees had wintered there,
Prisoning sugar in the virgin wax.

At times of transition,
Spring and autumn,
Their vibration swelled the room.

Laying his hand against the plaster
In the late May sunrise,
He felt the faint frequency of their arousal,

Nor winters later, burning the beeswax candle,
Could he forget his tremulous first loving
Into the humming dawn.[76]

Interesting that it references bees, just as Didsbury did in 'The Barn'. And like 'Lifted' and 'Prayer', it uses a rather everyday register of language, accurate and serviceable but not fancy. There is nothing not to understand here. The delicacy with which the facts are revealed is craft turned into art. Poems that are destined to be carried into our lives often speak quietly. When they whisper we listen harder.

'Towton' by Stanley Cook is another poem I read regularly. Like so many poets I have grown to admire, he was relatively unknown (if not mostly unknown) and only after his death did enthusiasm for his work start to build, culminating in the publication of his *Collected Poems*.[77] His publisher recommended it to me and I suspect he even gave me a free copy. It is a poem of reflection. In plain language, having laid out the facts, it dares to draw a conclusion about what the Battle of Towton might reveal about our species and its work in the world.[78] The final eight lines of this thirty six line poem are brutal in their frankness:

from *Towton*
by Stanley Cook

... Perhaps in a way it was saddest
Not that son killed father and vice versa
In the melodramatic early Shakespearean style
And not that former friend killed former friend
But saddest that, as usual, men killed strangers,
Mercenaries, turncoats and husbands
Of widows and fathers of orphans
Meaningless to those who did a job on them.

Cook took a risk with his use of the word 'saddest', which at the time he used it – and still now – had been drained of meaning through over-use. And his repetition of 'killed' is a blunt instrument that becomes sharper with use. As the full poem reveals, it is not written *in memoriam* but as an analysis of the buying and selling by a ruling class of the life and death of many others. It is Brechtian. Ekkehard Schall would have read it well.

The opening line of the second poem in Greg Leadbetter's sequence 'Dendrites and Axons', about his father's last years, reads: 'The horse came apart as you drew her –'. It is bold and devastating and it has stayed with me. I watched my own dad make slightly less sense of the world as he approached death and I see my mum increasingly unable to make the shapes she wants from her days, and so this line will not leave me. The complete poem, even taken out of its sequence, is chillingly precise.

from *Dendrites and Axons*
by Gregory Leadbetter

The horse came apart as you drew her –
mismatched perspective, split between the Fuseli head
and something that looked like a pig's rear-end.
This was early enough for a nervous joke
from someone – but though you never said as much,
this was your test, and you knew.

At the hospital, you had to draw a pentagon.
Geometry itself broke open: where
there should have been one, you drew
three, which overlapped like a Venn diagram.

An epicentre in the white space: chaos
in its blossoming fractal.[79]

Like so many of the poems I take with me, it is exact and uses just the language that is required. It also has in common with these other poems a sense of having been written after great thought, a careful struggle to discover what language was required to say what had to be said. It is thoughtful. None of these poets draw attention to themselves. They do not need to. They refuse to. When the poet steps back from the poem he or she invites the reader to step forward, to make their own relationship with the poems. Poetry needs space to work.

69 *The Classical Farm*, Bloodaxe Books, 1987. But also in *Scenes from a Long Sleep: New & Collected Poems*, Bloodaxe Books, 2003.

70 Deely boppers are an Alice-band with two glittery plastic stars on springs, for a time popular with small girls attending pantomimes. I like them too.

71 *Kith*, Nine Arches Press, 2015

72 I've worked many locks in my time, mostly while crewing for Jo Bell as it happens. They call it lock-wheeling and the thing you use to open the paddles on the lock gates is a windlass. But you knew that.

73 It is ok to simply love poems.

74 Anvil Press Poetry, 1993.

75 I realise that this isn't a maxim that is much heard amongst the general populace, mainly because I just made it up, like, now.

76 From *The Honeycomb*, Bloodaxe Books, 1989.

77 *Woods Beyond a Cornfield: Collected Poems*, Stanley Cook, Smith|Doorstop, 1995.

78 The Battle of Towton took place on Sunday 29th March, 1461 (using the Julian calendar) during the Wars of the Roses.

79 From *The Fetch,* Nine Arches Press, 2016

CHAPTER 8

Leicester Polytechnic invests in a Compact Disc player – Geoffrey Hill's Mercian Hymns *– Arvo Pärt's 'Cantus in Memoriam Benjamin Britten' – Jasper Carrot's brush with greatness – A note is received via a third party – W S Graham's 'The Nightfishing' – Cornish Herrings – 'The quay night bell' – Words cast into the silence.*

In 1986 I came across, by chance, a recording of Geoffrey Hill reading his book-length poem *Mercian Hymns.* The library at Leicester Polytechnic's Scraptoft Campus had just taken delivery of some CD players and what looked like a random selection of CDs.[80] One CD was of some of the mid-career work of the Estonian composer Arvo Pärt, including his *Cantus in Memoriam Benjamin Britten.* I listened to this at least once a week for a couple of years. Like the poetry of Miroslav Holub and Marin Sorescu, here was art from the middle of a Europe still under Soviet influence. It was mysterious and exciting. Another CD turned out to be a recording of Geoffrey Hill reading *Mercian Hymns.* I was unaware that the text had been published, I didn't know who Geoffrey Hill was, but I had a sense that he had things to teach me, about phrase-making and verse-speaking and the matter of England. Although I couldn't hear them simultaneously, Pärt's music became the soundscape to Hill's poem. A curious juxtaposition and why we will always need libraries.

The opening stanza sets out the issues to be considered and begins to reveal Offa's character:

from *Mercian Hymns*

By Geoffrey Hill

King of the perennial holly-groves, the riven sand-

> stone: overlord of the M5: architect of the historic rampart and ditch, the citadel at Tamworth, the summer hermitage in Holy Cross: guardian of the Welsh Bridge and the Iron Bridge: contractor to the desirable new estates: saltmaster: money-changer: commissioner for oaths: martyrologist: the friend of Charlemagne.

'I liked that,' said Offa, 'sing it again.'

Years later I persuaded the BBC Radio Producer Tim Dee that *Mercian Hymns* would make wonderful radio. He called my bluff by suggesting we offered the idea to BBC Radio Three with me being the one to do something with the text to make it more than just a reading. Tim was a highly regarded producer with many programmes to his name and I was a person who thought more people should hear this long poem. It was a good combination.

We pitched the piece with the idea that it needed to be heard through several voices (in the end it was three) and that a soundscape would be made to help carry the poem quickly into the imagination of the listener. Even with the facility to listen again – some way in the future at that time – radio has to make itself understood at first hearing. There's no turning

back the page to re-read a line. I proposed a complicated audio script placing the listener in a variety of relationships with the text. Leaving nothing to chance, we also suggested that as *Mercian Hymns* was clearly an homage to the West Midlands (amongst other things) we might approach Jasper Carrott, the Birmingham comedian, to be King Offa. The programme was commissioned but either Jasper Carrott wasn't available or his agent didn't get back to us or we forgot to ask him.[81] Either way, Offa's part was played by Simon Russell Beale with the rest of the text carried by David Bradley and Sonia Ritter.

Our permission to use the text was with the understanding that the words would be used exactly as written. We also decided there should be no words to introduce or explain the poem. Although King Offa is a dominant voice in *Mercian Hymns* other voices surface, including a narrator of sorts and what is perhaps Offa as a child. And as the piece is constantly shifting its setting and viewpoint – from 6th century Mercia to 20th century West Midlands – it seemed reasonable to offer the listener three voices that suggested competing spirits and memories, both reliable and unreliable. The adaptation was executed with a pair of scissors, a glue-stick and a photocopy of the poem taken from my copy of Geoffrey Hill's *Selected Poems*.[82] This allowed me to assemble – while maintaining absolutely the order of every phrase – the text that I felt should be spoken by each of the three voices. The challenge then was to make a soundscape that would be a counterpoint to the words. I was, in effect, writing a second poem to be heard alongside Geoffrey Hill's. I knew that what was described in the text did not need to be echoed with a sound affect, but something could be offered to help the listener more immediately understand the text. The finished piece plunged the listener from the skies above Mercia to the intimacy of King Offa's chamber, from Birmingham New Street Station to children leaving my son's primary school. The piece finished with the final minute of Arvo Pärt's *Cantus in*

Memoriam Benjamin Britten, a bell being struck and its note echoing into the distance.[83]

The piece was broadcast at 11.30pm on BBC Radio Three but managed to attract listeners, including Geoffrey Hill. He sent a note a few weeks later, mysteriously via a third party, to say he liked what we had done.[84] That was good enough for me and Tim. He added that we were at liberty to work with any of this poetry in the future.[85] Ten years later it was used as a sound installation in St Martin's Church in the Bullring in city-centre Birmingham as part of the Birmingham Literature Festival – the piece played unannounced at 4pm every day for a week with a succession of slides of pictures of the West Midlands projected up onto the ceiling.[86] And finally, a few years later, the Aldeburgh Poetry Festival *narrow-cast* it in a dimly lit room as an event. Twenty or thirty of us sat looking towards the speakers, trying to recreate the experience of hearing it alone at home or while driving or anywhere but with others. It was not unsuccessful, but listening with strangers in the same room is not radio as we know and love it. Radio is being alone, communally alone, but alone.

Adapting W S Graham's long poem 'The Nightfishing' was more challenging.[87] I had come across it in his *Selected Poems*[88] in the early 1990s and found myself still troubled by it twenty years later. It is early Graham, published in 1955. It is based on his experience of being taken out into the Atlantic on a Cornish herring fishing boat, but carries other concerns.[89] I approached the adaptation of this poem for radio with the knowledge that I was not certain I knew *exactly* what it was about, but I thought it should be heard late at night over the airwaves. It reads beautifully, with the precise musicality that suggests it should not be spoken like common speech, although not exactly sung either. Although written as if in one voice I found a form of dialogue in the piece so I gave it to a male voice and a female voice, described in the final production as just Woman and Man.

I struggled to make it work. I don't think Graham was a poet who had explicit designs on the listener or reader. He didn't write poems that would have won competitions (I doubt he'd have entered anyway).[90] He takes you so far and then you are on your own: reading, listening, thinking. I didn't have the nerve to just offer the text to the radio audience, even with different voices involved. I was concerned to leave them asking too many questions or waiting for too many answers. As is often the case, without the poet and all the excitement he or she brings, the poem must work very hard, must be really strong to stand on its own two feet. Not every poem gives itself easily. My solution, of sorts, was to acknowledge the difficulty by sharing it with the listener. I introduced a third voice with new words, spoken around the text – but not within it – as a dramatic commentary. My producer, Tim, added the aural suggestion that the reading of the poem was being recorded even as it was being broadcast. This was to be a private recording just like those private recordings of W S Graham I had heard in the 1980s.[91]

Here is the start, with production notes in square brackets and then the spoken text:

SCENE ONE

[Silence. Then sound of a 'record' button being pressed as on a reel-to-reel tape recorder.]

READER: To release 'The Nightfishing' two voices have been introduced, each able to speak from different viewpoints. These voices can alternate at will, triggered by the text or in order to help release the text. Rather than following the literal journey of the fishing boat out into the night, we follow the writer's journey to various places in his life. These include a stone cottage not far from the sea, where he is hunched over a manual typewriter, and also the shipyards of Greenock, public houses, poetry readings and finally a fishing boat.

This seems rather gauche now, but something was needed to lift the poem into the airwaves and at least the artificiality of the process was being acknowledged. The opening passage is a soundscape leading into the first lines of the poem:

[So, a man is sat in a rocking chair, dozing and rocking as he waits for the time to leave his cottage and go down to the fishing boat in the harbour. He holds the pocket watch to his ear so he will not forget time. Then, with a sigh, we hear him stand up, walk to the door, lift the latch and step out. As the door is briefly open we hear the world outside, including again very faintly some seagulls. The door closes and we are back to the room's silence. From inside that silence she speaks, slowly and firmly, sounding out every consonant.]

WOMAN: Very gently struck
The quay night bell.

We were, effectively, allowing everyone – the actors, the narrator and the listener at home – to step away from the idea of poetry being a spontaneous outpouring and to place it instead within all the artifice that is the making of radio. The actors Siobhan Redmond and David Rintoul took the voices of the Woman and the Man. I read the Reader's part.

Here's another extract:

READER:	Late evening air, the MAN walks downhill. His boots crunch. A breeze comes off the sea. He speaks quickly, urgently, holding the line breaks hard, keeping the verse structure in check.
MAN:	Now within the dead Of night and the dead Of my life I hear My name called from far out. I'm come to this place

And here is the final five line stanza:

MAN:	So I spoke and died. So within the dead Of night and the dead Of all my life those Words died and awoke.

Although Graham can't have meant the last phrase to have any connection with poetry on the radio, they describe the challenge. The words will die almost as soon as they are broadcast, within moments, and be followed by more words and the listener listening and processing and storing and assessing what meaning might be arrived at, and in doing so the words are awake again in these many minds. That is what radio does, casts the words out into the silence with no guarantee of anything but the *possibility* of something.

[80] All this and free lectures and a grant to be there.

[81] This is one of the great missed cultural opportunities of our time. He would,

actually, have been strangely excellent, with or without his moped.

82 *Selected Poems* by Geoffrey Hill, Penguin Books, 1985.

83 A reviewer suggested that featuring this piece was a bit clichéd. Well, yes, but sometimes we need cliché.

84 BBC Radio Three, 10th April, 2000.

85 I don't know why it never crossed my mind to take him up on this offer.

86 It caused some confusion and surprise to church visitors.

87 Again, with Tim Dee and broadcast on BBC Radio Three on 10th November, 2010.

88 *W S Graham, Collected Poems 1942 – 1977*, Faber, 1979.

89 *The Nightfisherman: Selected Letters of W S Graham*, Edited by Michael & Mary Snow, Carcanet, 1999, provides some background and *Where the People Are: Language and Community in the Poetry of W S Graham*, a study by Matthew Francis, Salt Publishing, 1998, also adds to our understanding of Graham's work and practice.

90 So many great poets are simply not 'competition friendly'. Do they not want to be the best?

91 Ronnie Duncan had played me cassette tapes he had made of his friend W S Graham reading his poetry. They were roughly recorded in back-rooms a decade or so earlier. Hearing them changed my life.

CHAPTER 9

The English Civil War & the Nicaraguan Revolution – Poetas del mundo – Festival Internacional de Poesía de Granada – A lake and a little brass band – Rubén Darío – Amplification – Ernesto Cardenal – Some fine examples of headgear – A poetry parade down to the lake – Fotógrafo: Recogedores de manzanas, 1981

England is far away from the centre of world poetry which, I discovered a few years ago, is Nicaragua. In this small Central American country with a turbulent recent history poetry is important. Nicaragua may not be any better or worse for its involvement with poetry but poetry is at the heart of the country in a way that it might once have been in England. Andrew Marvell and John Milton would have recognised some aspects of Nicaragua in the 1970s.[92] The poetry, war and revolution that transformed the country in the 20th century were peculiarly English things in the 17th century. They deposed a dictator, we executed a king. Spending even a short period of time in Nicaragua, as I did a few years ago, changed my view of what poetry might do in the world. It did this not just by allowing me to experience a celebration of poetry inextricably bound to politics but by hearing English as it is for millions of people, which is a little language possibly on its last legs.

In February 2014 I found myself as one of twenty people

in a shallow boat being propelled at speed across a small corner of a lake.[93] Around us were other boats on the same journey and still more would follow, carrying perhaps one hundred *poetas del mundo*[94] and a few relatives and friends. The waters were calm but ran deep. Some people were wise-cracking in Spanish, others stared into the middle distance. As we approached an island we heard the familiar sound of the little brass band that had been accompanying our every move for days. They played jaunty tunes and made us feel special. And here they were. It was the last day of the seven days of the *Festival Internacional de Poesía de Granada* in Nicaragua and we had relaxed into our roles. Language united us and divided us, although the one fifth of the poets who didn't speak Spanish were still diligently attending every reading, soaking up the sound if not the sense. We were clearly out of our depth but determined to enjoy the experience. We had found enough fellowship from across the seventy-one countries represented to feel that although we were not at the centre of this world, we were in orbit around it.

So much of my poetry life had, up until this point, been concerned with the minutiae of putting poetry into the world – how to pronounce correctly the Scottish towns featured in W S Graham's poetry, learning the words of poems by heart, attending to every beat in the bar – and here I was suddenly at the other end of the spectrum, at a festival that seemed to concern itself very little with details but simply stood four square in the world's way and got itself noticed. Quite possibly there are other poetry festivals that effortlessly take over a small city, but *Festival Internacional de Poesía de Granada* was like nothing I had ever attended. It took the aspirations and practicalities of presenting poetry in the UK and did exactly the opposite.[95] It was simply good sense. With a climate like Nicaragua's no one is going to hunt out the back room of a pub or a local library. Although Nicaraguans love shade they want sunny shade or a warm night. The poetry readings were outdoors in the evenings and in most cases presented in Granada's city square, in front of the Cathedral, making the poetry visible and public. It would have been impossible to sell tickets in such a setting, so goodbye box office income. The practicalities would have defeated the most diligent of venue managers and more to the point, in Nicaragua, for all its divisions and inequality, poetry is for the people. While the guest poets and dignitaries sat in reserved seats close to the stage, the rest of the audience were packed tightly around them, sitting and standing, motionless and milling around. They were free to come and go. They came and went.

Having a free event in the centre of a city is not usually a *guarantee* of audiences, but here it seemed to be. It was helped by the fact that after every poetry reading (and these lasted up to three hours) there would be a popular singer or a well-known band performing – but people were certainly there for the poetry. The poetry, by the Latin American poets at least, was spoken calmly and quietly, while the amplification flung it into the night sky. If something can be amplified the Nicaraguans will amplify it. The parakeets are very noisy and the ice-cream sellers ring their bells incessantly, but poetry must be heard. And poetry must be seen as well, so there were two large screens either side of the stage. The northern European convention of quiet poetry, quietly spoken in quiet places to small audiences would have seemed ridiculous here. The poets did speak quietly but their quietness was made loud. The audience's concentration was palpable. There were no corners cut when it came to making sure everyone heard every word. This was quite a responsibility for the poets, for their voices to fill a city square full of attentive strangers. No one was going to give applause if it had not been earned.

The poets were older, on average, than we'd be used to in the UK. At one of my three readings I was the youngster of the group at (then) a sprightly forty nine. The others, from Central and South America, perfectly rigged in smart-casual outfits with a range of well-made hats, were all in their sixties or seventies, possibly older. Rosabetty Muñoz from Chile, Harold Alvarado Tenorio from Colombia, Marco Martos from Perú, Adriano Corrales from Costa Rica, Luis Rochas from Nicaragua, senior citizens all. Perhaps age gave them wisdom and perhaps their poetry was wise, although it was hard to tell with very few translations into English. Content aside, they demonstrated how to read poetry the Latin American way. Their approach was to have confidence in the words, to cut out the chit-chat, to make no apology, and at no point try to entertain the crowd. That would have been undignified. They had dignity. In the course of the Festival, across dozens of hours of poetry, I did not hear a single indication of enjoyment from the audience other than the applause that followed concentration. Even the nodding of heads and murmurings of appreciation at the end of the poem, the default response of UK audiences, was absent. This was not, to resort to the hollow phrase beloved of poetry event promoters in the Anglo-sphere, a place of entertainment. But still they stayed, the audiences. Stayed and listened. Listened then applauded.

The Festival that year was in honour of Nicaragua's national poet, Rubén Darío (1867 – 1916). It transpired that everyone in Nicaragua, and most poetry readers across Latin America, knew his work. As my Nicaraguan poet friend, Francisco Larios, explained, Darío was such a well-known and well-loved writer, so important for the self-respect of the country, that every Nicaraguan child with even the remotest interest in writing – and that was many it seemed – wanted to be the next Rubén Darío.[96] In his lifetime Darío immersed himself in the world, active as a poet and writer, but also a diplomat and traveller, as at home in London or Madrid as in Granada or Managua. While this has never been exactly *uncommon* in UK poetry (there are examples of poets who rode various horses, including Andrew Marvell) being a poet doesn't seem to confer a status on a poet that might make them seem fit for other purposes. In Nicaragua, as the Festival demonstrated, there was a belief that if a man or woman (but sadly, still far too often a man) could write fine poetry then it followed that their intellect would be of use in the wider world, that they could possibly see more clearly what needed to be done, that they were more understanding of the frailties of our fellow citizens and therefore better able to rise above and to represent the people, all of the people. This is not a view promoted by opinion formers in the UK. This is not government policy.[97]

I am very likely romanticising a festival, a writing culture and a country that I do not well enough understand. However, one of the guest poets – in this case a special guest – had certainly found himself as a writer unable to retire to his chaise longue with a bottle of absinthe and a delicate constitution. Ernesto Cardenal was a Catholic priest and a published poet who found himself increasingly at odds with the regime of the Somoza family in the Nicaragua of the 1960s and 1970s. In his efforts to defend the poor and powerless he became a leading figure in the revolution led by the Sandinistas. His earlier poetry wasn't written with an expectation of a public but he responded to the revolution by writing long, detailed documentary poems, to explain and record what was really going on in a form that, thanks to the efforts of Darío and others, would be appreciated by a wide cross-section of the population, and certainly not just the literate and educated. Poets are eminently peripatetic but poetry is even more so. A good poem can move across a country – memorised, recited, referenced – at a speed to outflank even a well-equipped repressive regime. And of course, unlike ordinances, decrees, declarations and the Riot Act, poetry takes strength from speaking between the lines, from saying one thing and meaning another, from coming up behind figures of authority. As Tom Paulin reminds us in his poem 'Where Art is a Midwife'[98]:

There are things called ironies,
Also symbols, which carry meaning.
The types of ambiguity
Are as numerous as the enemies
Of the state.

In Cardenal's case, he believed that poetry could at least *help* make something happen. He was like Brecht in that respect. And when the revolution had started he stayed to try to see things through, joining the government, serving as their first Minister of Culture from 1979 to 1987. He could have stepped back into the literary shadows. He didn't. Inevitably, as a politician, he fell out with others and not everything went well, but when many years later he read his poems at the Festival, a rather frail old man, with an Old Testament beard and the obligatory revolutionary's beret – the silence was reverential. He was an example of poetry applied to life.

Cardenal's reading would have been part of a typical session at the *Festival Internacional de Poesía de Granada,* lasting up to three hours and featuring as many as twenty five poets, each reading only two or three poems. We formed a temporary poets' commune and in this spirit there was no sense of anyone being a headline act.[99] The most vivid expression of this egalitarianism was in the carnival, a parade lasting four hours through the city of Granada with poets reading from a platform on the back of a pick-up truck at every corner – amplified of course – to crowds of thousands packed into the narrow streets that stretched down to the lake. I read a poem of mine in rough Spanish – after hours of rehearsal and direction from the Costa Rican poet José María Zonta – and they cheered me although not much could be heard over the music and cacophony of the city. Here is the poem, without translation because I like the contrast between its southern English setting (varieties of apple trees, an elderly lady orchard owner, the hills of my beloved north Berkshire) and the Spanish language. It is translated by Katherine M. Hedeen and Víctor Rodríguez Núñez:

Fotógrafo: Recogedores de manzanas, 1981

by Jonathan Davidson

Huerto pequeño y recogedores de manzanas.
Cuatro jóvenes del pueblo,
seis aldeanas y un viejo,
el jardinero, memoria de cómo eran las cosas,
y la dueña, la señorita Balcombe,
madre soltera de los árboles.

Estoy parado junto a la carretilla.
Una chica se sienta allí, perdida en la luz,
sus pantalones de pana ajustados al cuerpo como corteza.
Las aldeanas entrelazan los brazos.
El viejo aguanta una pala.

La señorita Balcombe sonríe
con esa sonrisa de manzana salvaje.
Y detrás de nosotros, los buenos árboles:
de Laxton, de Bramley, de Wyken Pippen.
Hojas a gran escala se agitan en un vendaval
de North Berkshire,
raíces gruesas penetran la marga fértil, alcanzan la arcilla,
se mantienen firmes para la temporada.

Regresé el año pasado: se habían ido,
los manzanos, la gente.

Towns in the Northern hemisphere have plenty of parades and singing and dancing, but this was different because the attraction – along with bands and troupes of dancers – was actually the poets; shambling, perspiring, confused group though we often were. They cheered the poets of the world. And to remind us that there are battles still to be fought and that poets should take up their pens to change things, the festival that year had a focus on women's rights, and at the head of the carnival procession was a horse-drawn hearse carrying a coffin in which we were to collectively bury violence against women and girls by casting it off into the lake. The reading on the following night was by women poets, a gesture towards equality although regrettably the old male poets still outnumbered the women poets in the Festival. Jane McKie from Scotland read, along with Doris Kareva from Estonia, Rita Dove from the USA, Merja Virolainen from Finland, Fatina Al-Gurra from Palestine, Blanca Castellón from Nicaragua, Renata Bomfim from Brazil, Silvia Guerra from Uruguay, Sonja Manojlovic from Croatia and Anat Zecharya from Israel.

I name them because the names we know become the grid references we use to position ourselves in the poetry world. I had spent the best part of my reading life carving into the granite several hundred names to provide the hand- and toe-holds necessary for me to clamber about the cliff face of poetry. But despite my interest in those who were relatively unknown, the geomorphology I had created was Anglo-centric. In Nicaragua in the space of a week I was covering the globe with the gold stars of the poets I had met, and South and Central America glittered. I was still rooted in the British Isles but my centre of gravity was edging offshore. It was an education to mention to my new non-British poetry friends the names of the big-hitters over in the UK. One or two had heard of Ted Hughes, a few of Carol Ann Duffy (but only those in mainland Europe), the rest, despite their books and prizes drew blank looks. And to add to this alienation effect, within a few days of hearing so much poetry in Spanish and in so many other languages, English was starting to sound rather quaint. It was strange but not unpleasant, pale and potentially interesting, a language that didn't get out much.

The sound of poetry being read in Spanish must have been similar to how poetry had originally sounded to me as a child being read to by my mum. I had begun to recognise words from the rudimentary Spanish lessons that had allowed me to parrot my own poems in translation, and I was starting to hear the patterns of sound, perhaps even the shapes of the poems. The poets who read in their own languages before being translated into Spanish included Estonian and Hebrew and French and German and Arabic, so it was possible to start to hear how their languages offered differences and similarities. There may have been abstruse references and the subtleties of local colour, but first there was the music of the dancing syllables. With sufficient time a poem in Portuguese echoes a poem in Finnish and mostly, unexpectedly, it was the revealed silences that gave them kinship. What *Festival Internacional de Poesía de Granada* reminded me, as I had recognised as a child, is that it is the silences that create whatever shadow poetry casts. The spaces in which we wait and think.

92 Poets and politics, basically.

93 Lake Nicaragua, one of very few lakes in the world to have freshwater sharks.

94 Poets of the world!

95 I believe this was their motto: 'let us do it as the English would not'.

96 His poetry was available in the airport bookshop in Managua. And not only his poetry, lots of poetry, in Spanish and English. Stanstead it was not.

97 However, during a television interview in 2016 it was revealed that Jeremy Corbyn had a copy of a Bloodaxe Books anthology – possibly *Staying Alive* – on his bookshelf.

98 From *The Strange Museum,* Faber, 1980

99 Although the American poet Rita Dove was the non-Nicaraguan special guest, a great poet and with her husband an excellent dancer, both Latin and Ballroom.

CHAPTER 10

'Johann Joachim Quantz's Five Lessons' by W S Graham – A flute teacher – 'A young man with talent' – Karl is late and then Karl is early – The 'little creator' and the 'big creator' – Some herrings – A warning about chilblains – Strong drink is taken – Frederick the Great – We are not the art – Do not expect applause – Silence.

'Johann Joachim Quantz's Five Lessons' by W S Graham is not a poem that many people have come across. Graham wasn't ever terribly well known. When he was alive, in his later years, some people thought he was dead. When he was dead, the story goes, some thought he was still alive. He lived a long way from London and we should suppose that the many hadn't thought to call round to check. I have been reading the poem, one of his best but also not typical of his work, for over thirty years because it is not only exceptionally well made as verse but it carries ideas about art and poetry which offer a practical philosophy.

Ostensibly 'Johann Joachim Quantz's Five Lessons' describes a music teacher instructing a rather uncouth young man, 'a lout from the canal', in the playing of the traverse flute. It is set at some point in the 18th century and somewhere in mainland Europe, perhaps in the Netherlands or in one of those Hanseatic towns on the Baltic coast with their brick Gothic cathedrals and water-side warehouses. Quantz, the music teacher, was a real person with a well-documented life. He was tutor to Frederick the Great and a composer. He wrote the seminal work on playing the flute. It contains more than Five Lessons and if you are not a flute player it is a struggle to read. Graham's poem, by contrast, is a delight.[100]

Johann Joachim Quantz's Five Lessons

by W S Graham

The First Lesson

So that each person may quickly find that
Which particularly concerns him, certain metaphors
Convenient to us within the compass of this
Lesson are to be allowed. It is best I sit
Here where I am to speak on the other side
Of language. You, of course, in your own time
And incident (I speak in the small hours.)
Will listen from your side. I am very pleased
We have sought us out. No doubt you have read
My Flute Book. Come. The Guild clock's iron men
Are striking out their few deserted hours
And here from my high window Brueghel's winter
Locks the canal below. I blow my fingers.

The Second Lesson

Good morning, Karl. Sit down. I have been thinking
About your progress and my progress as one
Who teaches you, a young man with talent
And the rarer gift of application. I think
You must now be becoming a musician
Of a certain calibre. It is right maybe

That in our lessons now I should expect
Slight and very polite impatiences
To show in you. Karl, I think it is true,
You are now nearly able to play the flute.

Now we must try higher, aware of the terrible
Shapes of silence sitting outside your ear
Anxious to define you and really love you.
Remember silence is curious about its opposite
Element which you shall learn to represent.

Enough of that. Now stand in the correct position
So that the wood of the floor will come up through you.
Stand, but not too stiff. Keep your elbows down.
Now take a simple breath and make me a shape
Of clear unchained started and finished tones.
Karl, as well as you are able, stop
Your fingers into the breathing apertures
And speak and make the cylinder delight us.

The Third Lesson

Karl, you are late. The traverse flute is not
A study to take lightly. I am cold waiting
Put one piece of coal in the stove. This lesson
Shall not be prolonged. Right. Stand in your place.

Ready? Blow me a little ladder of sound
From a good stance so that you feel the heavy
Press of the floor coming up through you and
Keeping your pitch and tone in character.

Now that is something, Karl. You are getting on.
Unswell your head. One more piece of coal.

Go on now but remember it must be always
Easy and flowing. Light and shadow must
Be varied but be varied in your mind
Before you hear the eventual return sound.

Play me the dance you made for the barge-master.
Stop stop Karl. Play it as you first thought
Of it in the hot boat-kitchen. That is a pleasure
For me. I can see I am making you good.
Keep the stove red. Hand me the matches. Now
We can see better. Give me a shot at the pipe.
Karl, I can still put on a good flute-mouth
And show you in this high cold room something
You will be famous to have said you heard.

The Fourth Lesson

You are early this morning. What we have to do
Today is think of you as a little creator
After the big creator. And it can be argued
You are as necessary, even a composer
Composing in the flesh an attitude
To slay the ears of the gentry. Karl,
I know you find great joy in the great
Composers. But now you can put your lips to
The messages and blow them into sound
And enter and be there as well. You must
Be faithful to who you are speaking from
And yet it is all right. You will be there.

Take your coat off. Sit down. A glass of Bols
Will help us both. I think you are good enough
To not need me anymore. I think you know
You are not only an interpreter.

What you will do is always something else
And they will hear you simultaneously with
The Art you have been given to read. Karl,

I think the Spring is really coming at last.
I see the canal boys working. I realise
I have not asked you to play the flute today.
Come and look. Are the barges not moving?
You must forgive me. I am not myself today.
Be here on Thursday. When you come, bring
Me five herrings. Watch your fingers. Spring
Is apparent but it is still chilblain weather.

The Last Lesson

Dear Karl, this morning is our last lesson.
I have been given the opportunity to
Live in a certain person's house and tutor
Him and his daughters on the traverse flute.
Karl, you will be all right. In those recent
Lessons my heart lifted to your playing.

I know. I see you doing well, invited
In a great chamber in front of the gentry. I
Can see them with their dresses settling in
And bored mouths beneath moustaches sizing
You up as you are, a lout from the canal
With big ears but an angel's tread on the flute.

But you will be all right. Stand in your place
Before them. Remember Johann. Begin with good
Nerve and decision. Do not intrude too much
Into the message you carry and put out.

One last thing, Karl, remember when you enter
The joy of those quick high archipelagoes,
To make to keep your finger-stops as light
As feathers but definite. What can I say more?
Do not be sentimental or in your Art.
I will miss you. Do not expect applause.

In the First Lesson, Graham has Quantz say: 'It is best I sit / Here where I am to speak on the other side / Of language'. What an interesting statement. We generally believe that language is somehow inside us or perhaps that we are inside it, but we do not see it as being something we are on the other side of. We consider ourselves fluent and even confident, able to choose the best words and we think very often that this is what we do. We are writers – many of us – and language is like putty in our hands, it bends to our will. Here, we are being told that language is a barrier, that it is about obfuscation as much as clarification. Graham touches on this idea frequently in his poetry. We can never quite say what we mean. Philosophers have thought about this a great deal. As a practical man, Graham spent much of his life trying to shape language in order to communicate states of being that were *beyond* language. If we write literature then this is what we will be doing. It's not easy. The flute is an instrument that imitates the human voice – it uses a similar mechanism to human vocal chords – and perhaps that is why Graham chose to use a flute teacher to give us these lessons on language. When he speaks of playing the flute he speaks about learning to write and why it is important to *want* to learn (to write) and how difficult it will be, and, tellingly in the second line, an announcement that 'certain metaphors / Convenient to us within the compass of this / Lesson are to be allowed'. That's good to know.

The Second Lesson, has a lovely sly phrase. Quantz, or Graham, (let's settle on Quantz-Graham) describes Karl, his pupil, as 'a young man with talent' and then adds, 'And the rarer gift of application'. Odd. Why would the gift of application be so rare? It is because to apply oneself to poetry or any art is to necessarily do without other things. Or at least W S Graham's life suggests this was his view. He lived so frugally, almost as far away from whatever were then the centres of poetry as it was possible to be.[101] He might well have allowed himself to be taken on relentless lecture tours or he might have taught at American universities or got himself involved in the BBC, perhaps middle-management on the Third Programme. He didn't do that.[102] He sat at a table with a portable typewriter and paper and pens and he wrote and looked out at the world and wrote more. For so many years. Like Graham himself, our lout from the canals is gifted but he also knows how to graft. And Quantz-Graham continues, saying 'You are now nearly able to play the flute'. Which is odd, also, because perhaps Karl thought he *could* play the flute – after all he'd had two lessons – just as we all think we can write, when in fact we are all only *nearly* able to write. And that is, of course, the best state to be in: still approaching genius, but never quite there. And then he offers us two magnificent sentences:

> Now we must try higher, aware of the terrible
> Shapes of silence sitting outside your ear
> Anxious to define you and really love you.
> Remember silence is curious about its opposite
> Element which you shall learn to represent.

As writers we are *being* an element that is opposite to silence. We are representatives. I like that. Quantz-Graham is reminding us that although the world is terribly noisy, actually we are simply placing words into silence. Before we speak there is silence. After we finish there is silence. We only have to fill the bits in between. How hard can that be?

In The Third Lesson, Quantz-Graham is annoyed because Karl is late. It is extraordinary that anyone would ever be late for anything that concerned the study of art, including writing, but evidently it happened in the 18th century. And because Karl is late Quantz-Graham is not feeling too pleased with him. Again, who would have thought that a teacher of music – or of practical literature – might feel aggrieved at a student arriving late? Quantz-Graham says to Karl, 'You are getting on. / Unswell your head.' For those of you who are inclined to pin inspiring phrases above your desks, this is one I'd recommend. But Quantz-Graham is quickly forgiving of his student and asks him to play a piece of music – shall we say read a piece of writing – and says particularly: 'Play it as you first thought / Of it in the hot boat-kitchen'. Another lesson for us. Write it as you first thought of it. Which doesn't mean, I think, *don't* re-draft, but rather try to draft back to the original thought, or perhaps to let the original thought be released through you, with only the moderation that is required for it to sit sweetly in the ear.

We're over half-way through the poem. In The Fourth Lesson young Karl is early. Quantz-Graham rewards him for being prompt by offering him a phrase which can only be described as an absolute belter. He says:

> What we have to do
> Today is think of you as a little creator
> After the big creator.

Now it doesn't really matter what beliefs we have, the world has been created in some way or other, and we are the little creators coming afterwards. It's a responsibility, being 'a little creator'. And then he says, to Karl:

> But now you can put your lips to

The messages and blow them into sound
And enter and be there as well.

Whether we know it or not we all have messages for the wider world – or we do if we are writers – and when we write we are blowing them into sound. That's such an apt image for what we are doing as writers, giving voice, making the unheard heard.

At this point in the poem, they sit down together and have a drink, a glass of Bols as it happens. I am no advocate of alcohol as part of the educational process, but sometimes it is necessary for the teachers and the students to sit down together and take strong drink, or at least a cordial of some sort. And in the same lesson Quantz-Graham has said to Karl: 'You must / Be faithful to who you are speaking from / And yet it is all right.' The structure of the sentence is confusing. 'Be faithful to those you are speaking from.' It doesn't quite make sense to my mind. Well, it does if we recollect that a line or two earlier Quantz-Graham has acknowledged how much Karl likes the great composers ('I know you find great joy…'). I take it that he is suggesting that just as we are inspired by those great writers who came before us, and just as we will to some degree be channelling what we can of their genius, so we will in some counter-intuitive way be being heard by them, being read by them, considered by them, and we must be faithful to the art that has flowed through us all, that flows forever. An impossible notion. And therefore possible. And then, to conclude The Fourth Lesson, there is some stuff about the canals unfreezing as spring arrives and a timely warning about chilblains. Would that more creative manuals took the time to offer such useful advice.

And now we arrive at The Last Lesson. And low and behold, Quantz-Graham floors poor Karl with the announcement that this is to be his *last* lesson. It turns out Quantz has been given the opportunity to live in a certain person's house and tutor him and his daughters on the traverse flute. The fact is, he was off to teach Frederick the Great how to knock out a pretty tune, but more importantly for us is the realisation that at some point we will be on our own. As writers. At some point all the people who gave a damn about our writing will have faded away and we'll have to look after ourselves. Our friends and neighbours, our relatives and tutors, our enemies even, care about our work but they cannot care forever. That's another lesson. We should prepare to be alone with our writing.

In this Last Lesson there's a lovely description of Karl as 'a lout from the canal / With big ears but an angel's tread on the flute'. And Quantz-Graham says that at some point Karl will be invited in a great chamber to perform in front of the gentry. And he says, 'I / Can see them with their dresses settling in / And bored mouths beneath moustaches sizing / You up'. This happens. Writers are a curiosity but not particularly important to most people. Then in the last eight lines of this last stanza, Quantz-Graham gives it us with both barrels. Firstly he says: 'Do not intrude too much / Into the message you carry and put out'. That's the second reference to messages and he reinforces this idea that we are the medium, carriers, vehicles for the releasing of meaning. In fact he seems to suggest that the meaning is not ours it is just something that we carry. That's a thing to consider, that we as writers are a means of communication as much as originators. We carry, perhaps, the messages of our humanity, but we are not individually much beyond being simply well-played instruments. What we compose is only what we are provided with. The genius of the sculpture is as much in the stone as in the artist.

Then Quantz-Graham says: 'Do not be sentimental or in your Art'. Sentimental is troubling as the meaning changed considerably from the early 18th century to modern times. The Enlightenment saw it as referencing an outpouring of emotion as evidence of a good heart but by the end of the century Schiller had divided poets into naïve and sentimental with his vote going for the naturalness of the former.[103] Even if we assume Graham isn't giving Quantz a knowledge of the contemporary meaning he is definitely saying keep your emotions in check. The phrase 'in your Art' is more difficult. Having picked up a lot of the Quantz-Graham character by now – for all that this is a poem about writing it is also a beautiful character study, as good as Hill's portrait of Offa in *Mercian Hymns* – I favour him meaning that the creator or performer should locate themselves slightly outside the playing area of their artistic endeavour. Step back from the poem and let the words do the work, as I have heard myself say repeatedly. We are not the art.

The poem finishes with my favourite phrase. Quantz-Graham says to Karl, his last words to him: 'Do not expect applause.' I think 'expect' is the key word here. If you are expecting applause I understand and I commiserate. Applause is seductive. It can be well-deserved. It sometimes isn't. This is art, not entertainment. We, the audience, will be polite and even appreciative and we will applaud, but for those who are making and sharing work, you do the art-form a disservice if receiving the approbation of the multitude looms too large in your consciousness. It is Gonzagoan poison in your ears whilst you sleep. 'Do not expect applause. There is a sardonic humour to this that poets acknowledge (often by laughing out loud), but also I think key to the meaning is 'expect'. Having made the thing with words we should then expect what is its opposite'

[100] Reproduced by permission of Rosalind Mudaliar, the estate of W S Graham. Published in *W S Graham, New Collected Poems*, Ed. Matthew Francis, Faber, 2004. There is also an audio recording of Graham reading the poem on SoundCloud.

[101] The village of Madron in Cornwall, not far from St Ives.

[102] He did a small amount of all the things writers can do to supplement their living but never let his focus be anything but poetry.

[103] *On Naïve and Sentimental Poetry*, Friedrich Schiller, 1795.

ACKNOWLEDGEMENTS

My thanks to the many publishers, poets and copyright holders who have given permission for their poems to be used in this book. My thanks to Natasha Carlish and her colleagues at the Arvon Foundation for allowing me to spend a week writing in The Clocktower at The Hurst (the John Osborne Arvon Centre) during April 2016. My thanks to Ieva Balode and her colleagues at the Ventspils Writers and Translators Centre in Latvia for awarding me a writing residency for the month of June 2017. My thanks to Lisa Peter for reading and advising on early drafts of this work.

We are grateful to the following publishers and other copyright holders for permission to reprint poems as detailed below;

Ivan V. Lalić (Translated by Francis R Jones) 'The Spaces of Hope', from *The Passionate Measure*, Anvil Press Poetry 1989 / *Centres of Cataclysm*, Modern Poetry in Translation/ Bloodaxe Books 2016.

Miroslav Holub (Translated by Ian Milner) 'The Door', from *Poems Before & After: Collected English Translations*, Bloodaxe Books 2006

Ted Hughes 'Wind', *The Hawk in the Rain*, Faber 1957
William Dunlop 'Landscape as Werewolf', *Here Today*, Hutchinson 1963

Walter de la Mare 'Won't', *Poems*, Puffin Books 1962

Basil Bunting, extracts from essays; *The Poet's Point of View*, Bloodaxe Books 1966 and Preface from *Collected Poems*, Bloodaxe Books 1968. Both reprinted in *Briggflatts*, Bloodaxe Books 2009.

Ted Hughes 'Full Moon and Little Frieda', *Wodwo*, Faber 1967

Jenny Joseph 'Bonfire', *Rose in the Afternoon and other poems*, J M Dent & Sons Ltd 1974

Roy Fisher 'Linear', *The Long and the Short of it: Poems 1955-2010*, Bloodaxe Books 2012

Ian McMillan 'Platform 2', *To Fold the Evening Star: New & Selected Poems,* Carcanet 2016

Maura Dooley 'Dancing at Oakmead Road', *Sound Barrier: Poems 1982-2002*, Bloodaxe 2002

W S Graham 'Lines on Roger Hilton's Watch' and 'Johann Joachim Quantz's Flute Lessons', *New Collected Poems*, Faber 2004

Jackie Kay 'Darling', *New & Selected Poems*, Bloodaxe 2007

Brendan Kennelly 'Begin', *Staying Alive*, Bloodaxe Books 2002

Tony Hoagland 'Romantic Moment', *Unincorporated Persons in the Late Honda Dynasty*, Graywolf Press/*Being Human*, Bloodaxe Books 2010

Peter Didsbury 'The Barn', *The Classical Farm,* Bloodaxe Books 1987

Jo Bell 'Lifted', *Kith*, Nine Arches Press 2015

Carol Ann Duffy 'Prayer', *Mean Time*, Anvil Press Poetry 1993

Pauline Stainer 'The Honeycomb', *The Honeycomb*, Bloodaxe Books 1989

Gregory Leadbetter 'Dendrites and Axons', *The Fetch*, Nine Arches Press 2016

Geoffrey Hill, 'Mercian Hymns', *Selected Poems*, Penguin Books 1985